Managing Your Own Career

Dave Francis is a writer and consultant on management development – a social scientist turned businessman. He runs Richmond Consultants Ltd, which works internationally on top team building, management development and career management. He is the co-author of six other books, including *The Unblocked Manager* and *Fifty Activities for Self Development* (both with Mike Woodcock).

Dave Francis is a member of the Association of Teachers of Management and a Fellow of the Institute of Directors. He lives in Richmond, Surrey.

Other books for The Successful Manager

Manage Your Time Sally Garratt
The Roots of Excellence Ronnie Lessem
Managing Yourself Mike Pedler and Tom Boydell

Dave Francis

Managing Your Own Career

Fontana/Collins

First published in 1985 by Fontana Paperbacks,
and simultaneously in hardback by Collins,
8 Grafton Street, London W1X 3LA

Hardback edition ISBN 0 00 217610 6
Paperback edition ISBN 0 00 636872 7

Set in Linotron Times
Made and printed in Great Britain by
William Collins Sons & Co. Ltd, Glasgow

For my children
Samantha, Daniel and Gerald
as they launch their own careers

Contents

Introduction

This is a book for 'careerists': that is, those who want to manage their careers into the twenty-first century. My aim has been to write a down-to-earth guide for people seeking to improve the quality of their working lives.

If you're in early or mid-career, say between the ages of twenty-three and fifty-five with a track record of accomplishment, then you're the ideal reader for *Managing Your Own Career*. Most but not all of this book will be useful to those who are at school or college and are considering which career to start. Students and young people will need specific, additional information on career options, which this book does not provide.

Managing Your Own Career is a self-help package for those who wish to become more satisfied with, or more senior in, their work. People who are in a quandary about which career to follow, perhaps between jobs, will find the approach immediately relevant to career decision-making.

Books for careerists fall into two categories. First, there are those which focus on the individual by assessing personal wants, needs, talents and skills. The second category concentrates on the job market by giving factual information on different professions, trades and occupations, and listing entry requirements, prospects, and so on. *Managing Your Own Career* falls firmly into the first category: it provides a framework for gathering self-knowledge and improving career-building skills. Other authors have covered the descriptive field with great competence, and there would be no point in repeating here what has already been said so well.

Before we start thinking about managing our own career, it's useful to know exactly what we're talking about. According to the

Shorter Oxford Dictionary, a 'career' is a 'person's course or progress through life'. 'Management' is 'to control the affairs of, to administer, to deal with carefully, to bring over to one's wishes by artifice, to bring to pass by contrivance, hence, to succeed in accomplishing'. Accordingly, managing your own career is 'to carefully control and administer progress through life in accordance with one's wishes and achieve success'.

Although we have a definition of career management, the topic can be seen from different angles. For example, sociologists are interested in the relationship between individual careers and social change, while feminists may see careers as a facet of a male-dominated world; economists have yet another view since their interest is in examining the relationship between careers and wealth. Academic perspectives like these are not our concern in this book, which is solely devoted to helping individuals find and exploit career opportunities for themselves. *You* are the subject of the book; social, economic or political elements in career management are considered here only as factors which influence your career choices.

The concept of a career can be defined broadly or narrowly. For our purposes, the term means 'activities undertaken to earn a living'. So if you chose to give up a job as an architect and to become an art therapist, you'd be making a career decision, but if you decided to spend your evenings building matchstick models of the Taj Mahal, you wouldn't.

Activities which earn a living are interwoven with the total pattern of life, and this book approaches work in the wide context of love, health, family, fun, religion, and adventure. It is a holistic approach, considering a career as a form of self-expression which should integrate harmoniously into a whole lifestyle.

The philosophy of the book is: 'You must manage your own career: you can't depend upon anyone else to do it for you.' This principle emerged time and time again from the survey of fifty-three men and women who were interviewed to give the research base for *Managing Your Own Career*. Their career biographies gave invaluable practical guidance on the factors which lead to 'successful' or 'unsuccessful' careers.

The experience of survey respondents confirms that there is no formula which will provide you with a 'good' career. The aim is to find one that provides excellent 'fit' between who you are and what you do. Individual wants and needs vary greatly. For example, an apparently successful managing director may be totally dissatisfied with his jetset lifestyle and desire to move into a far less stressful occupation, while a middle manager may long to be promoted to a managing director's role. A secretary in her late thirties may find her work life meaningless and desire passionately to become a children's nurse, while a hospital nurse reflects on her demanding lifestyle and aches to be relieved of present pressures and responsibilities; she would cherish a well-paid secretarial job. Generalizing about successful careers in the abstract is fruitless, but working to find the right career for yourself is one of the most important things you can do.

Almost all of us face major career decisions at different points in our lives. Typical examples include women seeking to take up work again after having children, people made redundant in middle age, those who simply feel in a rut, and people who yearn to exploit their latent potential.

Having studied many career biographies I have come to believe, with regret, that a truly fulfilling lifelong career is a rarity. Few people seem to be either efficient or effective at managing their own careers. Why is success in a career such a minority sport? Partly because there is more human ability than society knows how to use, so many people are inevitably balked. Most importantly, those who fail to take a long-term perspective and early responsibility for their own careers are likely to end up disappointed. Young people often make fundamental decisions before they are able to realize the full implications of their choices. Career-building skills are well worth acquiring early.

I've learnt that people who genuinely want to stand out from the crowd and enjoy a richly satisfying career can't adopt a passive stance and believe that someone else will do it for them. Those who desire to use their work as a source of personal fulfilment are well advised to start early and to actively manage their own careers throughout their lives. Until recently, many people were able to delegate career management to an employer. In stable institutions this is still possible, but for most of us the rate of social and economic change means that organizations cannot take responsibility for our long-term career management, even if they wanted to. People sink or swim by their own efforts, although it's true that some set off with better buoyancy aids than others. In the last two decades, responsibility for career management has swung to the individual, and all indicators suggest that this trend will continue. At no time since the mass upheavals of the Industrial Revolution have so many people been made responsible for their own careers.

Since many people fail to enjoy careers which truly suit their desires and exploit their potential, we must ask: 'Is it possible to increase the probability of high career satisfaction?' The answer is: 'Yes, but . . . ' It takes willpower, specialized knowledge, skill and plain old hard work. In particular, it is essential to learn how to take sound decisions at key decision points. People who enjoy a 'good' career teach us that there are stances, attitudes, skills and competencies which help to fashion a better 'fit' between a person and their work. The purpose of this book is to convey insights from successful careerists in ways which will help you to increase the probability of better managing your own career.

Careers are dynamic and continue to be challenging throughout life. Someone who is fifty years old must make decisions as momentous as those faced by a youth of sixteen. In order to manage your career successfully, you'll need to have the capacity to change and grow psychologically until old age. New dilemmas occur throughout life. Unfortunately, people tend to become victims of habit, and close their minds to personal development. For years I've watched people attempting to change their lives, perhaps through willpower, therapy or academic study. I've learnt that although it's impossible for someone to change their nature, they can grow wiser about their true character. Personal growth must be continuous if people are going to be as dynamic as life around them.

Careers are a testing ground of character. Work can be an adventure which places people in new and demanding situations. Some are given opportunities to discover what kind of person they are, what they have to give, and what they want to receive. Others play out boring and stultifying work lives which stunt their personalities. I've been involved in human development for twenty years, and I'm still an optimist about people's capacity to grow and improve the quality of their lives. But this capacity doesn't come automatically.

There is a lot of scope for career development, but it isn't infinite. Not everyone can have high-flying careers. No matter how much an individual wants a particular role or achievement, there are objective limitations and constraints. A youth who is unable to sing in tune simply can't be an opera singer, and an intellectually dull man will never become a university professor. Ability is unevenly spread across the population. I can't believe in the Utopian notion that all boundaries are within the mind of man. Careers are built in the real world.

Finding the right career is a serious business. A 'good' or 'successful' career is the outcome of a struggle to fit personal needs, wants and capabilities into what the world has to offer. As my father, a tailor, was fond of repeating, 'You cut the best coat you can according to the cloth you have.'

Managing Your Own Career aims to be a helpmate in the lifelong preoccupation with the question of where you should invest your precious energies. It provides a structured investigation into personal needs, wants, motives and talents. You'll be able to identify how much, if any, frustration you have with your current job, and then you can adopt proven managerial techniques to 'carefully control and administer progress through life in accordance with your wishes'. And, hopefully, you will 'achieve success'.

All authors owe a great debt to others and although I can't begin to mention by name all those who have helped me, I thank them all. I particularly wish to express my grateful appreciation to fifty-three men and women who discussed their careers at length with me in 1984 and 1985. When I began to plan this book my objective was to help the average person – the man or woman sitting on the Clapham omnibus. In order to establish what ideas and techniques would be valuable I had to find out who was likely to be sitting on the bus, and what his or her career experience was like. So the idea of a survey was born. A London bus seats about fifty people. Could I find a representative busload who would act as informants? People willing to describe their career histories and aspirations were interviewed in a study which eventually consumed hundreds of hours. For brevity I call this the Richmond Survey or Study, since most of the discussions took place in my home. The respondents' dilemmas, successes and failures taught me an enormous amount. Brief biographies of those quoted in the book are given at the end of this introduction. Each respondent was interviewed for about two hours using 'historical patterning' and 'behavioural event' data collection methods. I should point out that the sample was relatively small and not properly representative of the population at large. For example, 'middle-class' careers received most attention and the majority of informants were British. For these reasons the results of the survey should be taken as illustrative, not definitive. The survey methodology was suggested by a published study of forty-four male graduates from the Sloan School of Management at MIT conducted by Professor Edgar Schein in the mid-1970s ('Career Anchors and Career Paths: a Panel Study of Management School Graduates' in Van Maanen (ed.), *Organizational Careers – Some New Perspectives,* Wiley, New York 1977).

I'd also like to thank all those who used preliminary versions of the questionnaires and projects described in this book. Their willingness to give feedback, which extended to the subtle nuances of wording, brought a level of clarity and precision that would not have been possible otherwise.

I acknowledge the help of two teachers, Roger Harrison and the late Dr A. Juer, who helped me to understand that self-insight and autonomy are vital and are the result of much hard work. Don Young also helped me greatly by introducing me to his powerful concept for defining the fundamentals of strategic management. He pointed out that there are three core questions:

1. What is my identity?
2. How can I direct my efforts successfully?
3. What capabilities do I need?

This simple but profound concept continues to evoke much useful thought. It was originally developed for corporate affairs, but its usefulness extends to individual career management.

In addition, the intellectual stimulation of Ben Tregoe and John Zimmerman who developed the valuable concept of 'driving forces' in their book *Top Management Strategy* (John Martin, London 1980) proved very fruitful. Also of great value was Edgar Schein's discovery of 'career anchors'. Henry Mintzberg of McGill University has been stimulating. I would like to thank Ezra Kogan and Jane Cranwell Ward for their valuable feedback on earlier drafts of the manuscript. I am grateful to Bob Garratt, the series editor, for suggesting that I was the right person to prepare this book. My daughter Samantha made a major contribution. Her precision and flair with the English language and her unfailing moral support have been very much appreciated.

Lastly I would like to thank my always helpful secretary, Monique Liesse, for typing and retyping the manuscript many times. The responsibility for the ideas and views expressed is, of course, my own.

Although any book is a snapshot in time, I hope that the *Managing Your Own Career* approach will continue to evolve. I'd like to ask you, the reader, for your help here. The validity of a book of this kind depends on whether it is useful to its customers; that is, the people who seek to manage their own careers. I would be grateful if readers would share their experiences with me so that I can improve later editions. Please write to me, care of Richmond Consultants Ltd.

The management of a career is a profound concern, equal in gravity to getting married or moving to a new country. I hope this book will directly help you enliven and refashion your career. The nineteenth-century philosopher Thomas Carlyle expressed perfectly the importance of a career when he wrote: 'Blessed is he who has found his work.'

Dave Francis
Richmond, Surrey 1985

The Richmond Survey

BIOGRAPHICAL DATA ON RESPONDENTS

NAME	JOB TITLE	DOMESTIC SITUATION	AGE
Alan	Managing director	Married (3 grown children)	56
Alison	Senior nurse	Single	29
Andrew	Financial director	Married (2 grown children)	37
Ann	Teacher	Married	47
Archie	Writer	Divorced (3 children)	43
Arthur	Electronics engineer	Married (2 children)	44
Baden	Managing director	Married (1 child)	36
Betty	Computer salesperson	Single	51
Bob	Solicitor	Divorced (2 children)	29
Caroline	Interior designer	Married (2 children)	28
Chris	Prison officer	Married (2 grown children)	47
David	Redundant draughtsman	Married (2 children)	39
Denese	Editor	Single (2 children)	36
Desmond	Freelance poet	Single	33
Don	Defence equipment salesman	Divorced	34
Frank	Engineering project manager	Married (2 children)	29
George	Redundant general manager	Married (1 grown child)	54
Harold	Carpenter	Married (1 child)	27
Harvey	Redundant manager	Married (2 children)	36
Jack	Shopkeeper (ex-actor)	Divorced (1 grown child)	56
James	Commercial director	Married	27
Jane	Housewife	Married (1 child)	18
Jerry	Entrepreneur	Married (3 children)	38
John	Catering consultant	Married (2 children)	32
Katherine	Marketing executive	Divorced (2 children)	36
Ken	Accountant	Married (3 children)	38

Louis	Business owner	Married (twice, 4 children)	41
Luke	Electronics consultant	Married (6 children)	32
Margret	Clerk	Single	31
Mark	Scientist	Single	28
Mary	Student	Single (1 child)	36
May	Teacher	Married (2 children)	41
Michelle	Clerk	Single	27
Mike	Airline pilot	Married	36
Norma	Film editor	Married (2 children)	31
Paul	Traveller	Single	27
Peter	Postgraduate student	Single	25
Petra	Personnel manager	Married	31
Ray	Army officer	Married	34
Richard	Priest	Married (3 children)	61
Robert	Unemployed	Divorced (2 children)	38
Roger	Civil engineer	Married (2 children)	32
Ruth	Actress	Divorced (2 grown children)	54
Salina	Buying assistant	Single	29
Simon	Electronic systems manager	Married (3 children)	34
Stephan	Journalist	Single	31
Tim	Doctor	Single	34
Tom	Distribution manager	Married (3 young children)	27
Tony	Company chairman	Married (2 children)	49
Walter	Personnel director	Divorced (2 children)	41
William	Production manager	Married (3 children)	38
Winston	Clerk	Single	23
Zia	Welfare rights counsellor	Single	41

(*Note:* names have been changed to respect the anonymity of respondents.)

How to Use This Book

Managing Your Own Career is a workbook. Please don't read it from cover to cover, like a novel, and then put it back on a shelf to gather dust. Use the book to provide a discipline, as a source of ideas, and as a guide and a goad. Remember how health enthusiasts took to aerobics in the early 1980s? Think of your author as a kind of Jane Fonda and the book as the aerobics of occupational fitness. As they say, 'Feel the burn!' Settle down, roll up your sleeves, and get ready: you're going to work on your career.

Every healthy person has a career, and that includes the prisoner in gaol, the street corner addict and the striptease artist. Careers have a fundamental impact on people's lives. They are the 'comeuppance' of personal decisions taken perhaps decades earlier. But how many people actually work hard at managing their careers? Nearly everyone worries about their future but only a few seem to take career decisions deliberately, progressively and appropriately. Negative decision-making, when the person appears virtually to abandon responsibility for managing his or her career, is commonplace. For most of us a career is created, not given. The world is not our oyster.

To a large extent we can choose whether or not to exploit our potential. Some Hollywood film actors and actresses remain superbly attractive into late middle age. Their secret is hard work. All those hours in the gym pay off with well-toned muscles and a youthful appearance. Most people don't take such good care of their physique, and they reap the ugly rewards of their neglect. Clarity, commitment and diligence are the time-honoured elements of success in fully exploiting our potential.

Managing a career demands a down-to-earth way of looking at

life, also vision and hope. The importance of imagination should not be underestimated. Someone somewhere in a run-down urban sprawl is dreaming of becoming a president, a millionaire or a missionary and, in twenty years, he or she will have achieved this aim. The youngster walks around town, kicking dustbins and playing ball, and creating the future in his or her mind. No one can pick out which of the grubby children will succeed but, somehow, a few will rise above the expectations embedded in their environment. Without imagination and vision, people become playthings of the banal repetitive patterns in their immediate world.

It is you, the reader, who must invest your imagination, hope, honesty and effort in the search for a career which suits you.

Notice that the comments refer to *you*. You are the one who has to slog to clarify what you want, who you are, what you can become, and how you are going to transform your aspirations into reality. There is hidden potential inside each of us, but this will remain obstinately latent unless it's exploited in the real world.

You need to understand the format of *Managing Your Own Career* before you proceed any further. You undertake a twelve-step review of the key dimensions which influence your career. The process follows a 'funnel' format. You start wide, and then narrow down to specific action plans. Each new step builds on previous work, with the overall aim of clarifying precisely what you should do to manage your career to best advantage.

Experience shows that at least twelve weeks is necessary for the complete self-study. You are asked to complete questionnaires, gather data, write, and talk; and, above all, to reflect and reflect and reflect. Piece by piece you develop a career management plan. It's rather like doing a jigsaw puzzle. The total time investment for the whole programme is one hour per day for ninety-four days: ninety-four hours.

Are you beginning to feel reluctant? Some people dislike structured approaches, which is understandable. It's a bit like school again, but if you feel that you want to skimp the programme, ask yourself: is it because you're unwilling to take your career seriously? Structured approaches are the best available methodology. Believe me, if there was an easier way I would give it to you. A logical, disciplined and reflective approach has proved to be effective.

A twelve-week project demands considerable investment of personal time and so it could disrupt your domestic life. Before starting, you're advised to discuss the approach with those close to you. Your spouse will have views. It's very important to have the support of others. Career decisions affect close family relationships, and the implications of one person's choice need to be considered in relation to the others who are involved. Some couples, for example, have undertaken the *Managing Your Own Career* programme together and developed imaginative and successful joint-career strategies.

Although this book is divided into twelve steps, or work packages, there are only three primary issues to be addressed. These derive from the concept that what really matters is to get a good fit between you and the world. The three key issues are interrelated and best shown in a diagram.

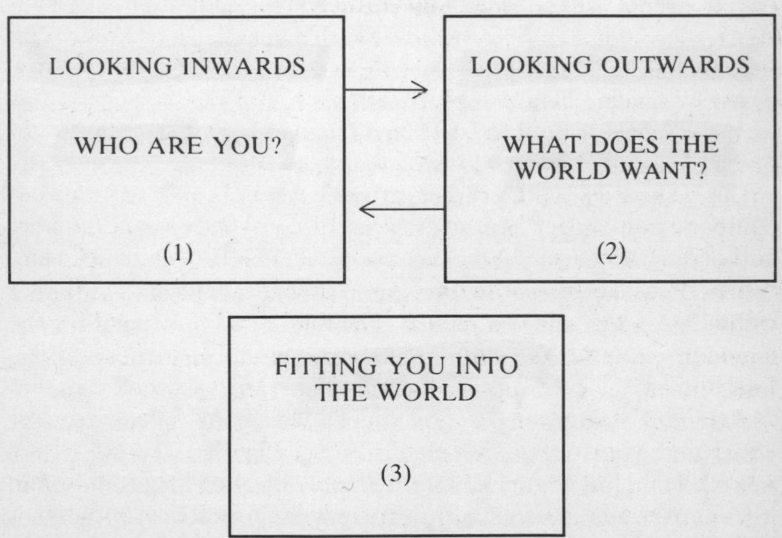

Consider the diagram for a moment. Box One looks inwards and considers who you are, what you want, your talents and constraints. Box Two looks at the outside world and examines what opportunities exist. Box Three fits you into the world. As you progress through the twelve steps, the perspective evolves: from self-study, through an examination of the environment, then finally into decision-making.

Each of the twelve steps addresses a core question:

PHASE ONE – LOOKING INWARDS

- Who takes your career decisions?
- What drives you?
- How effective are you?
- How satisfied are you?
- What are your talents?
- What constrains you?

PHASE TWO – LOOKING OUTWARDS

- What organizations suit you?

PHASE THREE – FITTING YOU INTO THE WORLD

- What are your long-term aims?
- What are your short-term objectives?
- How should you develop yourself?
- Should I make a career move?
- How can you exploit the present?

These twelve questions are complex and profound, requiring well-considered and individual answers. You'll consider each question in a weekly step which gives practical projects to be undertaken. The results and conclusions are recorded, so that *Managing Your Own Career* becomes a workbook. Week by week you evolve a personal action plan.

You'll find lots of checklists, questionnaires and suggestions, and it's worth repeating that full participation in practical projects is genuinely helpful. So get stuck in. It's imperative not to shirk analysis and reflection because these help you to gain new perspectives on your career past and future.

Each of the twelve steps begins with an explanatory section. Read this first and then undertake the projects suggested. Record your project results and complete each step by reading the interpretative material. Finally, re-read the explanatory section.

Undertake the steps in sequence, starting at the beginning. The process of analysis and reflection is cumulative. When you have completed all twelve steps, move into action and make the changes that your career review dictates. In the final analysis, career management is about change, not contemplation.

If you are a student, or someone out of the world of work, then two steps of this book may be irrelevant to you at the present time. These are Step Three which asks 'How effective am I?' and Step Four which looks into your present job. No problem. When you come to these steps just read the narrative and leave the projects until you have practical experience. But don't forget to resume the practical work in Step Five!

Now start your first project. Don't be shy! On the next page you will find Project Biodata. This collects basic facts about your life and career so far. Spend an hour completing the Biodata to give a foundation for the programme. Then you're ready to begin Step One.

BIODATA

Full name:

Age:

Parents' names and occupations:

Grandparents' names and occupations:

Family status *(include number and ages of children):*

State of health *(specify any physical limitations):*

Educational history *(give details of specialization, achievements):*

a. School:

b. Further education:

c. Vocational studies or specialist qualifications:

d. Short courses:

e. Any thesis, papers, presentations etc.:

Salary (now):

Salary history:

£50,000	
£40,000	
£30,000	
£20,000	
£10,000	
	1960 1970 1980

Foreign languages spoken/written:

Language *Fluency*

Professional societies etc.:

Sports, interests and hobbies:

Work experience record:
(Fill out a complete record of your experiences at work. Begin with the earliest and progress chronologically. Include all experiences which lasted for longer than one month.)

FROM (date)	TO (date)	JOB TITLE	RESPONSIBILITIES	EMPLOYER

Financial commitments:
(List your financial commitments in descending order, i.e. heaviest commitment ranks number one.)

	COMMITMENT	ANNUAL OBLIGATION
1.		
2.		
3.		
4.		
5.		

Stake in the world:
(List your possessions, and expected possessions such as family inheritances, in descending order, i.e. with the most valuable asset at the top.)

POSSESSION	VALUE

That concludes your Biodata project. Don't rush on. Look back over your notes and see what patterns emerge. Reflect on your history. When you feel ready, begin Step One.

Twelve Steps
to Your
Career Review

STEP ONE

Who Takes My Career Decisions?

> 'The fault, dear Brutus, is not in our stars,
> But in ourselves, that we are underlings.'
> *Shakespeare*

YOU ARE THE DECISION-MAKER

Slightly over 40 per cent of the people in the Richmond Survey said that they were experiencing a 'successful' or 'very successful' stage of their careers. I found that it was impossible to predict from someone's job history whether they would be content with their overall career progress. For example, Chris, a prison officer, and Desmond, a freelance poet, both felt pleased with their career choices while Alison, a senior nurse, and Stephan, a journalist, were profoundly dissatisfied, despite holding apparently interesting and challenging jobs.

The fortunate minority who were in a successful phase of their careers were asked: 'Why do you consider your career largely successful at the moment?' Most replied: 'Because I am doing what I really want to do.' Don explained this very well: 'My parents wanted me to go into something safe, such as banking, but I like people, status, travel and challenges. I thrive on pressures and novelty. Repetitive tasks bore me and make me degenerate into getting fat and depressed. After university I decided to look for a role which was fast-moving, impressive, international, pressured and social. It seemed to me that selling gave me the best environment, and defence equipment would give me the travel, prestige and rewards that I craved. Frankly, I am an achiever and I want to be on top. I joined a part-time Territorial Army unit and also studied sales techniques at college. I worked on my personality to become more acceptable, urbane and good to be with. I started looking for openings and eventually found an entry point in the defence industry.'

Don's case was interesting. Take a closer look at the way he worked things out for himself. He searched to find his motives and found a specific environment which suited him. Then, using all his guile and wit, he found a way of entering into his chosen work environment. Don's clarity and persistence were impressive and this began with a decision to oppose his parents' wishes. Now in charge of large defence contracts for a major company, he considers himself 'well satisfied', although he admits that 'I may want to find new challenges later in life.'

Don's biography provided a way to define 'success'. He had found a context that used his talents and gave him stimulation and rewards that were important to him. People like Don take responsibility for finding opportunities and 'load the dice' to get what they want. They bounce back after setbacks. To use the jargon of this book, they 'own' their careers.

Now reflect on those who said their careers were currently 'unsuccessful'. Their interview records are loaded with comments which show that most of them felt victims of malevolent circumstances. They had unfulfilled wishes and requirements, and were unable to transform their aspirations into reality. A gap between what they expected or desired and what they had actually achieved had become a source of distress which grew into general disenchantment and cynicism.

One career 'failure' story illustrates the need for aspirations which are grounded firmly in reality. Perhaps the most unhappy careerist in the survey was Michelle, a twenty-seven-year-old clerk, living with her parents in South London. She desperately wanted to be an actress but never entered the profession. Her room was crammed with books on the theatre, her walls covered with posters of the great Hollywood legends, and she read glamour articles on stars' lives voraciously. She said, 'I hate my office job, but there is no choice. I'm a failure, and I'm stuck. I'm totally frustrated.'

Michelle's parents and friends can only see her ambitions as wild, completely unattainable fantasies. Her clerical job has become the receptacle into which she dumps dissatisfactions from other parts of her life. She speculated that maybe she enjoys being a loser and finds perverse gratification in non-achievement. What is significant is that Michelle considers her career to be a 'failure' (her word, not mine). She has not:

1. Found out what she really wants and needs
2. Discovered her real strengths, non-strengths and weaknesses
3. Systematically developed her strengths
4. Worked hard to overcome her weaknesses
5. Used guile to find opportunities
6. Committed herself wholeheartedly to success
7. Attuned her aspirations to reality
8. Believed fully in her own capability

The Richmond Survey data strongly suggested that those people who rated their careers moderate or unsatisfactory had decided that the reasons were largely outside their control. The conclusion was obvious: these people felt that they were victims of their situation. I came to believe that the 'victim' mentality was the most common factor associated with unsatisfactory careers.

The ways in which people define their individuality to themselves (which we call 'self-concept') is vital to explaining success or failure from the point of view of the individual. This is, of course, highly subjective. The stances people took towards themselves varied greatly. Some people felt basically positive while others could not respect themselves at all. 'Self-concept' has a profound effect on all aspects of career behaviour. It even affects physical health and social relationships. Most respondents seemed to be almost unaware of the distinctive character of their self-concept, believing that their own values and views were totally objective.

I concluded, after examining many career biographies, that self-concept works against career management when there is a strong temptation to avoid taking full responsibility for one's own destiny. Perhaps this is because many of us yearn to be protected and we unconsciously look to families, astrology, religion, governments, community leaders or popular fantasies to direct us in life. In spite of the faith and dependence invested in these, I cannot find any evidence to suggest that adults thrive whilst depending on others to take care of them. We have to grow up and take control for ourselves: this is the only way to win. If we don't do this, we fail materially and morally.

No one in the Richmond Survey had a successful career handed to them on a plate. Although wealthy families provided stability and opportunity, they couldn't provide satisfaction. One respondent reminded me that a man born to be heir to one of Britain's merchant shipping empires chose to fulfil himself studying African rodents! From the survey sample, it seemed that successful careers were the fruits of assertive personal decisions based on hope, search, clear vision, developed capability, genuine realism, long-range planning and individual diligence.

What conclusion can we reach from this? There seems to be only one: that it pays to own your career. This means wanting to – and being able to – take responsibility for yourself. Responsibility is a key concept. The *Shorter Oxford Dictionary* defines the word 'responsible' as 'answerable, accountable, capable of rational conduct, reliable, trustworthy and of good credit and repute'.

Why was it that so many survey respondents felt unable to take full responsibility for their careers? They looked around them and saw the truth of Rousseau's remark: 'Man was born free, and everywhere he is in chains.' I heard many complaints about the failures of the government. It became clear that the capacity to be responsible does not come automatically; it must be learned.

A lot can be explained if we look at the degree to which the individual is self-aware. Early in life we begin to interpret the world in habitual ways and these patterns become etched deep into the landscape of our minds like river valleys scored through an arid landscape. Thoughts and actions follow well-worn paths and this undermines our capacity to be fully conscious of what is happening at the instant. Without self-awareness it is impossible for an individual to be genuinely responsible.

Responsibility for oneself includes questioning basic values. Most published career advice is about achieving self-satisfaction and self-aggrandizement. Such guidance has more to do with taking than giving. It was interesting that almost all of the 'successful' careerists in the Richmond Survey emphasized the importance of contributing to others. Tony, a company chairman, put the point especially clearly when he said, 'I have always considered pure self-seeking to be hollow motivation. Success is important but success for what? We feed off each other and should try to do what we believe is valuable. It is good for people to feel gratitude and give back the equivalent of what they have been given themselves.' Tony also observed, 'I consider my career to be a way of serving my fellow men. As I grow in power and position this becomes more and more important to me. Someone must try to make a positive impact on the world, there are enough people who don't give a damn.' The careerist should not neglect to discover what he or she wishes to contribute to others through work.

Can we learn to be more responsible for our own careers? The answer from the Richmond Survey would appear to be: 'Yes, but . . . ' The first step is to realize that it takes a long time. If you were asked to learn Sanskrit you would know straight away that it takes years of study before you become competent in the language. Taking responsibility for your own career is just as demanding, and you will need to make an equal commitment to learning and hard work.

Taking effective ownership of yourself is vitally important, but the understanding of this isn't new. The strength and importance of self-ownership is well understood by those who nurse seriously ill people. Let's take an example. Douglas Bader lost both legs in an aircraft crash before the Second World War, and, as he lay in hospital, semi-conscious and racked with pain, he overheard two nurses talking. One said: 'Keep your voice down. There's a boy dying in there.' At this point Bader decided that he would not die. He made an astonishing recovery and went on to a distinguished career as a fighter pilot, even managing to escape from a German prisoner-of-war camp in spite of having two artificial legs.

Willpower made the difference between life and death for Douglas Bader, and there are other examples which show the immense importance of personal choice and determination. In a 1984 study Dr Jeanne Achterberg reported that the survivors of cancer share a number of positive psychological traits, including a refusal to give up hope, a rejection of the role of invalid and a preparedness to consider new ideas. Such people had a powerful belief in themselves. Dr Achterberg said: 'These people denied bad news. They refused to accept their sickness. I don't think that they understood their limits.'

Many branches of medicine recognize the importance of awareness and choice. Doctors now accept that people can have a much greater degree of control over their bodily functions than was previously believed to be possible. It is now widely accepted that many patients with high blood pressure can reduce it using 'biofeedback'. This method involves helping them to become aware (with the aid of a sensitive feedback instrument) of inner conditions which increase blood pressure. Using this equipment, the patients can learn to control their own metabolism. These medical examples illustrate that with proper training and appropriate information it is possible to become aware and make choices about aspects of our lives which we previously thought to be beyond our control.

The Richmond Survey echoed the fact that we are the decision-makers. Even unconscious personal decisions condition the present and future to a much greater extent than we usually realize. Patients with high blood pressure need to find the inner triggers to control their own condition; careerists need to become aware of the impact of their decisions on their fortunes. The most important thing is to raise consciousness about who we are, and develop our potential to be genuinely decisive.

This isn't idealistic and impractical. Some people change their lives by becoming aware of their own desires. Ann gave up a senior job as a computer programmer to study art therapy. She said: 'I desperately wanted to do something which would have lasting value. So after a lot of heartache I decided to change the whole direction of my life.' However, for most of the people in our sample the constraints on being radical were keenly felt. They have spent so long in one lifestyle that change is threatening. Stephan, a journalist, explained: 'My hobby is gardening. I spent a couple of years laying out my garden and now the results are fantastic. I'd like to be a professional gardener, but I'm dead scared of making the jump.'

We must not see careers as theoretical exercises. They're not. We have to make bold, sometimes momentous choices. The simple but profound message that 'You're the decision-maker' is fundamental. All of us, whether we realize it or not, make profound choices which shape our lives. If we fail to recognize that we each own our career, we will lack the willpower to sculpt a career which fits our own personal wants, needs and capabilities.

Alan, a successful managing director, made the same point in a particularly vivid way. He said: 'I've learned to be a survivor despite being up to my ears in the brown stuff on many occasions. The secret is to rise above any situation and take a helicopter view. No one can have an effective career and run around like a rat in a maze. Perspective is everything.' The successful careerist seems to be able to stand outside opportunities and take personal decisions deliberately. Whatever choices are made, however, the careerist must adopt positive attitudes and seek to exploit every situation.

This fundamental principle, that responsibility rests with each person, is echoed by those who give advice on careers. Mike is a career counsellor in a company employing 700 people. He observed: 'I get people coming to me all the time and asking, in effect, "What is the company going to do to develop my career?" I have to answer, "Nothing!" The company simply won't develop anyone's career unless he happens to be the son of the chairman.'

We can conclude that passive or victim attitudes are poorly attuned to thriving in today's competitive world. The rate of economic, social and political change forces people to become guardians of their fates. Successful careerists act to take well-considered choices (ownership) and live by the outcomes (responsibility).

Now it's time to undertake a project. We'll begin by reviewing how far *you* have 'owned' the key career decisions in your life so far. Undertake the Career Decisions Project as suggested on the next page and record your conclusions. You've started! Good hunting!

CAREER DECISIONS SO FAR

This project helps you to evaluate who has 'owned' the basic decisions about your career so far.

What to do:

Obtain seven large index cards and copy one statement on to each card. The seven statements are:

1. **The following events/people have profoundly influenced my career decisions so far:**

2. **I have taken the following actions to review my career progress:**

3. **I am using my present occupation to prepare for the future in the following ways:**

4. **I feel proud of the following aspects of my career so far:**

5. **These are examples of the risks I have taken to further my career (give full details):**

6. **I have felt the master or mistress of my own destiny in the following situations:**

7. My career so far has contributed to others in the following ways:

Take a pencil, an eraser and the headed cards and go to a large park or the countryside and walk for at least an hour to relax. Enjoy the natural surroundings. Try to go somewhere unfamiliar where you can be anonymous. When you feel quiet in yourself, find a comfortable place to reflect and take out the cards. Jot down your answers to the questions but do not strain to be definitive. Simply capture the truth of who you are at the moment. Keep reviewing the cards, adding comments as they occur to you.

Repeat the exercise at least twice. Reflect on each question, continuously amending your answers to capture the truth, the whole truth, and nothing but the truth!

When you have formulated your best answer to each of the questions, it is useful to seek the comments of others. Select people who know you well and share your thoughts and feelings. Ask for their reactions and comments. After each discussion take a few minutes and update your notes. When you feel that all the questions have been thoroughly explored, write your final conclusions on the next page.

Career Decisions So Far: Conclusions

1. The following events/people have profoundly influenced my career decisions so far:

NAMES/EVENTS	HOW INFLUENCED?
1.	
2.	
3.	
4.	
5.	

2. I have taken the following actions to review my career progress:

ACTIONS	WHAT RESULTED?
1.	
2.	
3.	

4.

5.

3. I am using my present occupation to prepare for the future in the following ways:

	WHAT I AM DOING	HOW IT WILL HELP
1.		
2.		
3.		
4.		
5.		

4. I feel proud of the following aspects of my career so far *(be specific):*

1.

2.

3.

4.

5.

5. These are examples of the risks I have taken to further my career:

RISKS	WHAT WAS THE PAYOFF?
1.	
2.	
3.	
4.	
5.	

6. I have felt master or mistress of my own destiny in these situations:

SITUATION	WHAT WAS THE OUTCOME?
1.	

2.

3.

4.

5.

7. My career so far has contributed to others in the following ways:

1.

2.

3.

4.

5.

STEP TWO

What Drives Me?

> 'This above all: to thine own self be true,
> And it must follow, as the night the day,
> Thou canst not then be false to any man.'
> *Shakespeare*

INNER IMPERATIVES

When a wide range of career biographies are studied, we can see the emergence of interesting patterns. People's work lives differ greatly, but it is possible to detect consistent themes within each personal history. Fifty-one of the Richmond Survey respondents were over the age of twenty-five and all but three of these had a number of recurring threads running through their career histories. It was as if each one wove the fabric of his or her individual career but, like Scottish clan tartans, there were a limited number of predictable variations.

Careerists are energized by motives which drive them. If they are to be successful they must take forceful initiatives to increase the possibilities of getting what they need and want from their work lives.

What are these energizing and driving forces? In order to explain this we have to introduce the concept of 'career drivers' which are inner imperatives mobilizing people and shaping their careers. A career driver is an inner force which determines what you want and what you need from your working life.

Career drivers emerge from within a person and provoke action. They are a form of self-expression which says 'yes' to life. People informally understand the notion of career drivers; you'll have heard them described as 'interests' or 'concerns'. Alan, managing director of a substantial public company, demonstrated awareness of his career drivers when he said: 'I have always wanted to be in charge. At school I ended up running the drama society. Then decisions about further studying were based on my desire to be the guy sitting in the back of the Jaguar reading the *Financial Times*. I love being the man who makes the key decisions. I have always opted for responsibility. I can see myself being the Chairman of the Retirement Association after they put me out to grass. It's in my blood.'

Career drivers do not appear to be chosen consciously, but to derive from the individual's personality, abilities, values and self-image; they're revealed rather than selected. Slowly, adults learn who they are and what excites and fulfils them. Career drivers are the unseen hand which guides personal decision-making.

I first learnt about the role of driving forces in a perceptive book called *Top Management Strategy* by Ben Tregoe and John Zimmerman (John Martin, London 1980). Successful organizations are faithful to a single, clear strategic driving force. This concept is also valid for understanding career management. The implication is that each individual must identify, and take action to satisfy, his or her driving forces. Tregoe and Zimmerman said that an organization must look to key executives to determine its driving force. You, the careerist, must look within yourself. The career driver concept is similar to that described by Edgar Schein's pioneer work in the 1970s when he detected recurring themes which 'anchored' an individual to a particular line of work.

Career drivers proved to be an invaluable diagnostic device for understanding the patterns revealed by respondents in the Richmond Survey. Only personal criteria could be used to judge the worth and validity of career choices, so a good career can be defined as the extent to which the total experience meets individual wants and needs. Conscious appreciation of our particular career drivers helps us to take initiatives which really suit us. We are more able to follow the advice: 'to thine own self be true'.

A word of warning at this point: deeper understanding of your career drivers will clarify *what* you are looking for, but not *how* to achieve it. The purpose of identifying your career drivers is to illuminate the inner forces which are shaping your career, not to provide immediate solutions. At first, bringing career drivers into clearer focus may increase frustration as the gap between what is and what is wanted becomes more apparent.

However, despite temporary discomfort, identifying your own career drivers provides you with a valuable tool for self-management. The Career Drivers Survey beginning on page 50 is the vehicle to explore what drives your career. Step Three and Step Four develop the concept further.

Clarity about which career drivers energize you helps to give:

- Long-term perspectives (careers are lifelong so you need to raise your eyes from immediate preoccupations)
- Clarity (having a better knowledge of who you are helps you decide between 'yes' and 'no')
- Strength (bold statements release inner energy)
- Distinctiveness (identifying your own drivers enables you to stand out from the crowd)
- Coherence (the career driver concept organizes factors which are otherwise apparently disconnected)
- Protection (reduces the risks of haphazard decisions)
- Stimulation (provokes a different view of yourself)
- Monitoring (gives criteria to assess career progress)
- Common language (provides a framework for dialogue and enables you to discuss your career with colleagues, friends and family)

Without a framework for self-assessment the individual is at sea. In his interview Paul said, 'I have never understood why I do what I do. It is almost as if a psychological puppet-master pulls the strings of my life. I wish that I could find what really turns me on.'

Career drivers emerge from deep within the person, but this doesn't mean that they are unchanging or totally beyond the influence of the conscious mind. The Richmond Survey contained several cases which demonstrated that the driving forces which shape our lives respond to changing circumstances. One career case history makes the point: that of Louis, who had owned a chain of sex shops in northern England. He freely admitted that his motivation was 'purely financial'. He said: 'Personal profit was my sole objective. I used to walk around with a bundle of bank account books, all under false names.' Then an event changed his view of the world. He explained: 'I went abroad on holiday and happened to meet an American missionary. He helped me realize that although my life was lucrative, it was totally empty. I couldn't get the realization out of my mind. Eventually, I sold the sex shops and told the truth to the income tax authorities.' In the language of this book, Louis's dominant career driver switched. He later spoke of the importance of 'feeling at ease with my conscience'. He is now a successful businessman running totally legitimate enterprises.

Willpower is potentially capable of reshaping career drivers, but according to respondents, intellectual decision alone has little power to change a life direction. Zia, a sparkling but nervous lady in early middle age, said: 'I really must take the decision to settle down. Ever since I was eighteen years old, I have given up my job and travelled whenever I got the chance. This is spoiling my life and I know it. I get a job, settle in, and then some opportunity comes up, and I'm off again. I've wanted to establish a place in the world for years. I've tried to fight this wanderlust, but I have never managed to succeed.' Zia felt driven by half-understood forces that she could not control. A year later, as she learned to manage her career, she had found ways of reconciling apparently divergent themes. She said: 'Only when I came to understand what I really wanted could I begin to manage my career.' Zia's developing willpower helped her to curb her wayward desires and find a deeper level of satisfaction. She has found a role that satisfies her: she works as a welfare rights counsellor for old people.

A barrier that many of us come up against when we try to be true to our own career drivers is other people. All sorts of people have developed a desire to guide and influence our decisions. There is a wealth of evidence from social psychologists demonstrating that most of us are highly suggestible. A human being is open to influence from parents, lovers, family, friends, leaders and the hotchpotch of inputs that we call contemporary culture. Children's careers are frequently programmed by their parents and this can disguise their genuine drivers. For example, Harold was born with physical problems and his parents wanted him to take up clerical work, but he fought against their influence and did what he wanted: he became a carpenter. Harold said: 'I felt like a cat having its fur stroked the wrong way, so I said – politely – sod 'em.' Ken, an accountant, had a similar experience, and commented: 'My parents emphasized security. They wanted me to be 100 per cent sure of a middle-class job. So the professions were the number one choice. No one cared what I really wanted. It was just assumed that I agreed with their values. I didn't know any better, so I just fell in and became an accountant. My real nature is much more expressive and artistic.' Ken is making plans to enter art college as a mature student in two years when his children begin work. He bitterly regrets that 'I did what I was told, and not what was right for me'.

In general, suggestibility proved to be dangerous for members of the survey. Rather than being supported in becoming who they were, people tended to be manipulated into becoming someone else's ideal. I came to believe that career choices should emerge from inner drivers. This emphasized that careers begin with self-study. There is often a real risk of being seduced away from one's basic nature, which needs to be resisted.

The effective careerist must get to know those inner forces which shape his or her needs and wants. These define personal identity, give direction, and add momentum. The Richmond Study identified nine distinct career drivers. The following project for this step provides a technique to explore your own career driver profile.

CAREER DRIVERS SURVEY

Introduction

By now your appetite should be whetted. The preceding pages argued that there are consistent themes or drivers in careers which shape and guide life and work decisions. What are your drivers? How do they influence your career?

This project helps you begin to answer these questions. It asks you to relate thirty-six pairs of statements. The results, when analysed, provide your career driver profile.

A word of warning before you complete the questionnaire. Sometimes you will find yourself struggling to compare two items which appear equally relevant or irrelevant. But, please persist. The technique forces you to weigh difficult choices, and the discipline has proved worthwhile.

There are no right or wrong answers – it all depends upon personal preferences, so please be as honest and objective as you can. Work through the questionnaire quite quickly: ten minutes is usually long enough.

Instructions

Below are listed thirty-six pairs of reasons often given by people when they are asked about what they want and need from their career. You must evaluate the relative importance to you of the statements within each pair and allocate three points – no more, no less. In other words, the possible distribution of points between the two items in the first pair, for example, would be as follows:

choice one:	A = 3 points	B = 0 points
choice two:	A = 2 points	B = 1 point
choice three:	A = 1 point	B = 2 points
choice four:	A = 0 points	B = 3 points

The letters given before each item are for the purposes of scoring and need not concern you at this stage. Just make sure that when you have completed each pair three points have been given each time.

1. (A) I will only be satisfied with an unusually high standard of living.

   (B) I wish to have considerable influence over other people.

2. (C) I only feel satisfied if the output from my job has real value in itself.

   (D) I want to be an expert in the things I do.

3. (E) I want to use my creative abilities in my work.

   (F) It is specially important to me that I work with people whom I like.

4. (G) I would obtain particular satisfaction by being able to freely choose what I do.

   (H) I want to make quite sure that I will be financially secure.

5. (I) I enjoy feeling that people look up to me.

   (A) Not to put too fine a point on it, I want to be wealthy.

6. (B) I want a substantial leadership role.

   (C) I do that which is meaningful to me, even though it may not gain tangible rewards.

7. (D) I want to feel that I have gained a hard-won expertise.

   (E) I want to create things which people associate with me alone.

8. (F) I seek deep social relationships with other people in my work.

   (G) I would get satisfaction from deciding how I spend my time.

9. (A) I will not be content unless I have ample material possessions.

   (D) I want to demonstrate to my own satisfaction that I really know my discipline.

10. (C) My work is part of my search for meaning in life.

    (E) I want the things that I produce to bear my name.

11. (A) I seek to be able to afford anything I want.

    (H) A job with long-term security really appeals to me.

12. (B) I seek a role which gives me substantial influence over others.

    (D) I would enjoy being a specialist in my field.

13. (C) It is important to me that my work makes a positive contribution to the wider community.

    (F) Close relationships with other people at work are important to me.

14. (E) I want my personal creativity to be extensively used.

    (G) I would prefer to be my own master.

15. (F) Close relationships with other people at work would give me special satisfaction.

    (H) I want to look ahead in my life and feel confident that I will always be OK.

16. (A) I want to be able to spend money easily.

    (E) I want to be genuinely innovative in my work.

17. (B) Frankly, I want to tell other people what to do.

    (F) For me, being close to others is really the important thing.

18. (C) I look upon my career as part of a search for greater meaning in life.

    (G) I have found that I want to take full responsibility for my own decisions.

19. (D) I would enjoy a reputation as a real specialist.

(H) I would only feel relaxed if I was in a secure career.

20. (A) I desire the trappings of wealth.

(F) I want to get to know new people through my work.

21. (B) I like to play roles which give me control over how others perform.

(G) It is important that I can choose for myself the tasks that I undertake.

22. (C) I would devote myself to work if I believed that the output would be worthwhile in itself.

(H) I would take great comfort from knowing how I will stand on my retirement day.

23. (F) Close relationships with people at work would make it difficult for me to make a career move.

(I) Being recognized as part of the 'Establishment' is important to me.

24. (B) I would enjoy being in charge of people and resources.

(E) I want to create things that no one else has done before.

25. (C) At the end of the day, I do what I believe is important, not that which simply promotes my career.

(I) I seek public recognition.

26. (E) I want to do something distinctively different from others.

(H) I usually take the safe option.

27. (B) I want other people to look to me for leadership.

(I) Social status is an important motivator for me.

28. (A) A high standard of living attracts me.

(G) I wish to avoid being tightly controlled by a boss at work.

29. (E) I want my products to have my own name on them.

(I) I seek formal recognition by others of my achievements.

30. (B) I prefer to be in charge.

(H) I feel concerned when I cannot see a long way ahead in my career.

31. (D) I would enjoy being a person who had valuable specialist knowledge.

(G) I would get satisfaction from not having to answer to other people.

32. (G) I dislike being a cog in a large wheel.

(I) It would give me satisfaction to have a high-status job.

33. (A) I am prepared to do most things for material reward.

(C) I see work as a means of enriching my personal development.

34. (I) I want to have a prestigious position in any organization for which I work.

(H) A secure future attracts me every time.

35. (F) When I have congenial social relationships nothing else really matters.

(D) Being able to make an expert contribution would give me particular satisfaction.

36. (I) I would enjoy the status symbols which come with senior positions.

(D) I aspire to achieve a high level of specialist competence.

Scoring the Career Drivers Survey

To score the survey, add up all the points that you have given to each of the A, B, C, D, E, F, G, H and I items. Write the totals in the boxes below and check that the grand total is 108.

A		B		C		D		E	
☐	+	☐	+	☐	+	☐	+	☐	+

F		G		H		I	
☐	+	☐	+	☐	+	☐	= 108

Copy these scores on to the Career Drivers Profile on the next page.

Your Career Drivers Profile

Mark your scores on the chart below by circling the numbers you scored for each letter. Then join up the circles to give a diagrammatic profile of your personal career drivers. When you have done this, read the next section to interpret your profile.

24	24	24	24	24	24	24	24	24
23	23	23	23	23	23	23	23	23
22	22	22	22	22	22	22	22	22
21	21	21	21	21	21	21	21	21
20	20	20	20	20	20	20	20	20
19	19	19	19	19	19	19	19	19
18	18	18	18	18	18	18	18	18
17	17	17	17	17	17	17	17	17
16	16	16	16	16	16	16	16	16
15	15	15	15	15	15	15	15	15
14	14	14	14	14	14	14	14	14
13	13	13	13	13	13	13	13	13
12	12	12	12	12	12	12	12	12
11	11	11	11	11	11	11	11	11
10	10	10	10	10	10	10	10	10
9	9	9	9	9	9	9	9	9
8	8	8	8	8	8	8	8	8
7	7	7	7	7	7	7	7	7
6	6	6	6	6	6	6	6	6
5	5	5	5	5	5	5	5	5
4	4	4	4	4	4	4	4	4
3	3	3	3	3	3	3	3	3
2	2	2	2	2	2	2	2	2
1	1	1	1	1	1	1	1	1
0	0	0	0	0	0	0	0	0
A	B	C	D	E	F	G	H	I
MATERIAL REWARDS	POWER/ INFLUENCE	MEANING	EXPERTISE	CREATIVITY	AFFILIATION	AUTONOMY	SECURITY	STATUS

Now that you've completed the Career Drivers Project and recorded the results as a profile, you're no doubt puzzling over the results and trying to understand what they mean. First of all, let me remind you that a career driver is an inner force which determines what you want and need from your working life. Drivers are sources of energy and direction which become obvious as we study the shape of our working lives. The Richmond Survey suggested that many people are only dimly aware of their career drivers, and so they're tempted to take critical decisions based on other people's influence, or on mere expediency. Such choices often prove to be unfulfilling.

A career driver is more than a tendency or a predisposition. It is an inner imperative which strongly influences the individual. Those people who don't fulfil their drivers find it extremely difficult to come to terms with the loss. Wise individuals fight tenaciously to express their primary drivers. A career driver isn't just a superficial personality characteristic; it's a fundamental component of an individual's identity.

Research with the Career Drivers Project showed that most people have two or three major drivers with only one at the core. It's this key driver that guides career progress and gives coherence to apparently unconnected choices and decisions.

From analysis of the Richmond Survey data nine distinct career drivers were identified. Each is a blend of wants and needs, and although there is slight statistical overlap between some drivers you can think of them as being quite distinct. The nine career drivers are:

1. **Material Rewards** – seeking possession, wealth and a high standard of living
2. **Power/Influence** – seeking to be in control of people and resources
3. **Search for Meaning** – seeking to do things which are believed to be valuable for their own sake

4. Expertise	– seeking a high level of accomplishment in a specialized field
5. Creativity	– seeking to innovate and be identified with original output
6. Affiliation	– seeking nourishing relationships with others at work
7. Autonomy	– seeking to be independent and able to make key decisions for oneself
8. Security	– seeking a solid and predictable future
9. Status	– seeking to be recognized, admired and respected by the community at large

The concept of career drivers was amusingly illustrated by a friend who described the kind of holiday activity that an individual dominated by a particular driver would prefer:

Material Rewards	– improves a run-down house for sale at a profit
Power/Influence	– organizes the local scout camp holiday
Search for Meaning	– meditates in a Zen Buddhist temple
Expertise	– writes a book on career management
Creativity	– writes a book called *Love and War in 2010*
Affiliation	– joins ten other people on a sailing holiday
Autonomy	– prepares a presentation for his bank manager on opening a copyshop franchise
Security	– revises his portfolio of investments
Status	– acts as chairman of a local charity fund-raising appeal

Career drivers are enduring, but apparently not fixed for a lifetime; changes are provoked by new circumstances or personal insight. Remember Louis, who ran sex shops until he met an American missionary? Careerists should detect and respond to changes in their career driver profile. Data from the Career Drivers Project is a snapshot of today. I advise you to review your profile every few years or when your external situation changes.

Look through the more detailed descriptions of each driver in the remainder of this chapter. Then complete the Career Driver Profile Narrative on page 71.

THE NINE CAREER DRIVERS

1. Material Rewards: seeking possessions, wealth and a high standard of living

Material rewards are defined as tangible assets, including money, possessions, quality of housing, and other material possessions.

People with material rewards as a career driver take decisions about future work life primarily to enhance their material wellbeing. They seek roles which provide a high income, and they take on tasks which may be unfulfilling or uncongenial but which provide a high income or other material rewards. For example, they may move house or even emigrate only for material advantage.

Perhaps the ultimate example of people driven by material rewards is that of the fashionable 'yuppies' of America. These young upwardly mobile men and women are devoted to the pursuit of wealth. They are fastidious about their dress and possessions, and take enormous interest in investments, taxation and other financial areas of life. They have developed a distinctive set of ethics which value materialism above almost everything else.

An example of someone with material rewards as a dominant driver was Tim, a doctor, who decided to work as personal physician to an Arab family for three years. He said: 'It makes no sense from a professional or lifestyle viewpoint. The only benefit is that I'll end up with £200,000 in the bank and that will set me up for life.'

The key concern of this person is *wealth*.

2. Power/Influence: seeking to be in control of people and resources

Power/influence is defined as wanting to be dominant and to have others behave in subordinate roles. Also connected is wanting to take decisions about policy and how resources are expended.

People who have power/influence as a career driver take

decisions primarily to increase the extent of their personal control over people and situations. They attempt to move towards the centre of organizations and gain both formal and informal power. They get satisfaction from deciding what should be done and who should do it, and they're often uncomfortable in subordinate roles.

People with power/influence as a key driver seem to gravitate towards managerial or political roles. They're proactive (initiating), they use personal power, and they have high self-confidence and clear ideas about what should be done. They are concerned with impact.

An example of someone with power/influence as the dominant driver is Alan, the managing director of a major company. He's known to his subordinates as HI (Hitler Incarnate). He always insists on knowing exactly what's happening in all major areas of the business. He's affable, outgoing and very clearly 'the boss'. Despite his pervasive presence, Alan is greatly liked by his subordinates. He's respected as 'firm but fair'. Even senior directors check that their shoes are clean before they go into Alan's office. He takes care over the images of power: his suits are handmade in Harrods, and his personal Jaguar is always gleaming. He exudes 'presence'.

The key concern of this person is *dominance*.

3. Search for Meaning: seeking to do things which are believed valuable for their own sake

Search for meaning is defined as being motivated to do things considered to be a contribution to something bigger, finer or greater than the individual according to religious, emotional, moral, social or intellectual criteria.

People with the search for meaning as a career driver will take decisions which are explicable only in the context of their personal beliefs and values. This may take the form of helping others rather than helping themselves. Personal fulfilment is the ultimate payoff, and they may make considerable sacrifices in order to follow their inner beliefs.

The desire for meaning is sometimes connected with other career drivers. One of the most materially successful respondents in the Richmond Survey was Baden, a millionaire who continued to work despite his financial independence. When asked why he still spent fourteen hours a day at his desk he said: 'Basically, I'm interested in the use of power. I want to know whether power can be used beneficially in a large organization. I'm an elitist. I believe that organizations need to be run by those who are best suited to the job. I have strong morality, and I believe that I'm well suited to taking charge. Anyway, it interests me.' Baden was driven both by search for meaning and power/influence.

An example of someone with only search for meaning as the dominant driver is Mary. She spent most of her life as a civil servant but was constantly involved in self-exploration. She attended encounter groups, studied astrology, meditated, and read extensively in the mystical tradition. Two years ago, she gave up a secure job and joined a small clinic to teach social skills to deaf children. The senior physician used a holistic approach and lectured widely on the value of spiritual communication with the deaf. Mary is now impoverished as she has to pay all her own expenses, and she lives in a simply furnished room. Her bookshelf is crammed with poetic, spiritual and educational material. Her career future is uncertain, but this does not perturb her. She says: 'I am sure I am doing the right thing for me.'

The key concern of this person is *contribution*.

4. *Expertise: seeking a high level of accomplishment in a specialized field*

Expertise is defined as specialist knowledge, skills, knowhow, competence and capacity to perform unusual, difficult or specialized activities.

People with expertise as a career driver work hard to gain a depth of competence in limited but specified fields and will strive to maintain their specialist capability. They dislike going outside their defined area. One of their primary sources of satisfaction is being valued as an expert. The expertise may be mechanical, craft, intellectual, scientific or practical. So both a blacksmith and an accountant probably have expertise as a career driver. Professional managers can be included in this category, especially those with formal training in management sciences.

People driven by expertise structure their working lives around a defined discipline. The context and challenge of the work determines their behaviour. Generally, professional or trade qualifications are seen as essential entry qualifications. Since most disciplines are continuously developing, the specialist keeps up to date with journals, conferences, study programmes and so on.

An example of someone with expertise as the dominant driver is Tom. He now manages the distribution department of a petrol company, but when he was sixteen he left school in order to become a professional sportsman, playing several times for his country. While he was at school his interests were sporting rather than academic and he left school with poor examination results. Later a recurrent knee injury prevented him from continuing as a sportsman and he became a lorry driver. After a few years a supervisory job became vacant, and then he was promoted to depot manager. Now in charge of the distribution department, Tom has achieved a great deal: he runs an efficient team, he's made massive cuts in overheads and he's solved many industrial relations hassles. He's eager to move on, but he's decided not to stray from his new expertise as a distribution specialist. His aim is to become a distribution director in a medium-sized company. He will not entertain a move into general management. He says, 'I have found my niche in distribution. I know it and I'll stick with it. I feel confident that I can cope in distributive management.'

The key concern of this person is *mastery*.

5. *Creativity: seeking to innovate and be identified with original output*

Creativity is here defined as devising something new which bears the name of the originator. This may be a work of science, art, literature, research, architecture; an entrepreneurial activity or even a form of entertainment.

People with creativity as a career driver do things which are distinctly different from those which others do, and they want to own the results. The individual's name is closely associated with his or her products. Genuine innovation is very highly prized.

People driven by creativity derive excitement from breaking new ground. They're stimulated by puzzles, riddles, challenges and problems. They can tolerate setbacks or failures without letting them destroy optimism. A feeling of accomplishment in producing something novel is key. People with this driver are willing to take decisions which may result in disadvantage if it means they can work in creative ways. They often prefer a solitary or small team environment to large bureaucratic systems.

An example of someone with creativity as a dominant driver is Luke. As an electronics consultant he can earn excellent fees, but last year he chose to take three months off and go to Crete to try to resolve fundamental mathematical questions about the nature of certain electrical wave forms. The result was a highly technical paper read at a symposium in Hong Kong recently. Luke says: 'I didn't care whether I earned a penny out of the Crete venture. It was a challenge I just couldn't resist.'

The key concern of this person is *originality*.

6. *Affiliation: seeking nourishing relationships with others*

Affiliation is defined as striving to be close to others, enjoying bonds of friendship and being enriched by human relationships.

People who have affiliation as a career driver take initiatives to develop deep and fulfilling relationships with others. These bonds become extremely important to them. They put their feelings for others above self-aggrandizement and preserve continuity in important relationships. They may continue with unsatisfactory or unfulfilling jobs because of the quality of their relationships with others. Their commitment is to people, not to task, position or organizational goals.

An example of someone with affiliation as a dominant driver is Jane. Now eighteen and married to a butcher's assistant two years her senior, she lives in a council flat and has just had her first child. They are always hard up and life is very much a matter of coping with practical problems. Jane visits her Mum almost every day and other young mothers are always around. Along with her baby daughter there are two enormous dogs. The pop music that fills the flat, mingled with the sound of the television which is constantly on – whether anybody is watching it or not – is often drowned out by the barking of dogs or the squealing of infants.

Jane says, 'The only thing I really care about is having nice people around me.'

The key concern of this person is *closeness*.

7. *Autonomy: seeking to be independent and able to make decisions for oneself*

Autonomy is defined as taking personal responsibility for the structure, processes and objectives of daily life.

People with autonomy as a career driver act to increase the amount of control they have over their own working lives. They resist attempts by organizations to put them in boxes. They identify, and then fight, constraints. People like this often fail to cope well with bureaucracy and seek to become their own masters. They enjoy feeling 'I did it all', and they prefer to work alone or with a small team which they lead.

The desire for independence is very influential in autonomy-driven individuals. They do not like to be directed by others. They experience the procedures, systems, conventions and protocols of others as irritants. Restrictions evoke hostility or fury and their response is to create environments where the individual sets his or her rules. Sometimes such people can function happily in organizations where they negotiate a good deal of psychological space for themselves. This type of person would sacrifice organizational position for self-direction. There is survey evidence that those who are self-made are strong in this driver.

An example of someone with autonomy as a dominant driver is Jerry. A self-made millionaire at the age of thirty-eight, Jerry has many attributes. He's involved in many businesses, all of which are dependent on him. He loves to 'push back the frontiers', and have his own name on organizations which he controls. He puts himself forward to achieve results that others find difficult. An ex-boss said that he was the world's worst subordinate. Jerry has an insatiable appetite for personal achievement, saying: 'I want to have a little bit of posterity with my name on it.'

The key concern of this person is *choice*.

8. *Security: seeking a solid and predictable future*

Security is defined as wanting to know the future and to avoid being exposed to unpredictable risks.

People with security as a career driver take decisions which help them to feel relaxed about their future. Their primary goal is high predictability, rather than high income. They see life as a journey to be undertaken by the safest routes with the best maps and guides available.

This type of person chooses employers after careful consideration of their stability and record of looking after employees. They may associate security with membership of blue chip companies or institutions. They make career choices with the future in mind. If a promotion opportunity substantially increases doubt about the future, they may well reject it. People driven by security accept what the world has to offer rather than taking a radical stance; they evade conflicts which could become make or break. They undergo training to increase their worth to the parent organization. Until recently security was seen to be related to long service, but this is no longer always the case and the security-driven person may well move from organization to organization in order to build breadth of experience which results in increased personal marketability. This is seen as a 'bankable asset'. People like this are often considered conservative and company workers but their roles can be innovative and progressive.

An example of someone with security as a dominant driver is Mike, an airline pilot. At the age of fifteen Mike decided that he would be a successful and secure family man. He selected his career on the basis of predicted shortages over the next thirty years and took great care to join an airline with a policy of paternalism and respect for long service. He studied diligently, modelling his style on successful airline captains. He invests carefully to build a strong financial base. He said: 'Although the work bores me, I know that I have a totally secure income and that my privileges will stay intact. That's what matters to me and my family: a strong base.'

The key concern of this person is *assurance.*

9. *Status: seeking to be recognized, admired and respected by the community at large*

Status is defined as wanting the esteem of others, and to be highly regarded. Status is demonstrated by symbols, formal recognition and acceptance into privileged groups.

People with status as a career driver undertake whatever actions are needed in order to enhance their prestige. This includes making personal contacts with influential people, taking responsible assignments and self-publicizing. They may seek positions of power and authority, but their desire is for the prestige of the position rather than the exercise of control.

Status is not directly related to social class. For example, some people value being recognized as an authority on art or as a person with outstanding fashion sense. The person is motivated by a desire to impress others and be acknowledged as worthy or special.

An example of someone with status as a dominant driver is Ray, who is an army major. He is very conscious of social differences and is very concerned to make an effective presentation of himself. He does all the 'right things' by giving dinner parties, mixing with high-status people and being seen to be a man of substance. He said: 'I feel that it is important to be well-connected. Quite frankly, if one is accepted in the best circles then everything else turns out well.'

The key concern of this person is *position*.

CAREER DRIVER PROFILE NARRATIVE

Now that you've read the descriptions of the nine career drivers, it's time to reflect by writing down your conclusions. Complete below fifty words on each of your top three drivers, saying how each driving force has influenced your life thus far. Do this before moving on to Step Three.

Driving force one *(highest score)* TITLE ________________________

Driving force two *(second highest score)* TITLE ________________

Driving force three *(third highest score)* TITLE ________________

Technical Note

The author wishes to acknowledge the following writers in the field of personal development and career management whose published work contributed to the definition of each of the nine career drivers:

Material Rewards: F. W. Taylor, *Scientific Management*, Harper and Brothers, New York 1911, B. F. Skinner, *Science and Human Behavior*, Free Press, New York 1953; E. E. Lawler, *Pay and Organizational Effectiveness*, McGraw-Hill, New York 1971.

Power/Influence: D. C. McClelland, *Power, the Inner Experience,* Irvington, New York 1973; Richard E. Boyatzis, *The Competent Manager*, Wiley, New York 1982; D. G. Winter, *The Power Motive,* Free Press, New York 1973.

Search for Meaning: C. Argyris, *Personality and Organization*, Harper and Row, New York 1957; A. Maslow, *Toward a Psychology of Being*, Van Nostrand Reinhold, New York 1968; D. Levison, *The Seasons of a Man's Life,* Alfred Knopf, New York 1978.

Expertise: R. N. Ford, *Motivation through the Work Itself,* American Management Association, New York 1969; G. O. Klemp and L. M. Spencer Jr, *Job Competence Assessment,* Addison-Wesley, Reading, Mass. 1983.

Creativity: F. Hertzberg, *Work and the Nature of Man,* World Books, New York 1966; Danzig-Nevis International Inc., *Blocks to Creativity*, Cleveland 1970; D. C. McClelland, *The Achieving Society,* Van Nostrand, Princeton 1961.

Affiliation: D. C. McClelland, *The Achieving Society,* Van Nostrand, Princeton 1961; R. E. Walton, 'How to counter alienation in the plant', *Harvard Business Review,* Nov./Dec. 1972, pp. 50-70/81; J. W. Atkinson and N. T. Feather (eds), *A Theory of Achievement Motivation,* Van Nostrand, New York 1966.

Autonomy: A. Maslow, *Motivation and Personality,* Harper and Row, New York 1970.

Security: E. Schein, *Career Dynamics,* Addison-Wesley, Reading, Mass. 1978; H. Mintzberg, *The Nature of Managerial Work,* Harper and Row, New York 1973.

Status: V. H. Vroom, *Work and Motivation,* Wiley, New York 1964; R. Tannenbaum and W. H. Schmidt, *Social Psychology of the Work Organization,* Wadworth, Belmont, California 1966.

STEP THREE

How Effective Am I?

'O wad some Pow'r the giftie gie us
To see oursels as others see us!'
Burns

FEEDBACK ON YOUR ACHIEVEMENTS

Now you've drawn your career driver profile, but there's a small problem. Your views are inevitably subjective and the technique used assumes that everyone has the same quantity of drivers. Of course this is unrealistic. You really need objective data to validate your career driver profile. One very useful way of evaluating your profile is to collect feedback about yourself from other people. Though this is a potentially confrontational and sensitive procedure, it will help you to find out what you've achieved so far and to reach valid conclusions about your strengths, non-strengths and weaknesses.

Before you proceed with the self-study, it's worth asking: 'What is a strength?' From a careerist's viewpoint a strength has four aspects:

1. The skill to perform well
2. The willingness to perform well
3. The confidence to perform well
4. Recognition by others

The first three (skill, willingness and confidence) are qualities under the direct control of the individual, but the fourth (recognition) can only come from other people. Yet recognition is vital since it gives a licence to perform. For example, it may well be that a young man has the skill, willingness and confidence to direct a successful feature film, but someone with $25 million to invest has to recognize this before the young film-maker can use his first three abilities. For this reason we can only say that a strength exists when all *four* aspects are present.

Strengths open doors for us, while non-strengths close them. Why do I say 'non-strength' instead of 'weakness'? Because a non-strength is not necessarily a weakness. No single human being can excel in every area of life. Non-strengths only become weaknesses when they prevent us from meeting commitments or performing to an acceptable standard.

Our vulnerability to poor career decision-making is increased if we either underestimate or overestimate our strengths. Some people are, frankly, unrealistic. Robert, a respected senior supervisor in a manufacturing company, was made redundant with generous financial compensation. He had dreamed of running a shop, and his redundancy money gave him the chance to purchase a profitable motor accessory shop. Robert's expensive foreign holidays and negligent book-keeping attracted the insistent attention of the tax inspector and the business deteriorated. Formerly loyal customers went elsewhere, and Robert is now bankrupt, living in a dingy bedsitter and full of excuses for his failure in business. He says: 'Suppliers failed to keep their promises, and I was so busy that I didn't have time to keep the books straight. I really didn't get a fair crack of the whip.' The real facts are different. The truth is that Robert was lost when organizational disciplines were removed. Like many others before him, he failed to appreciate his strengths, non-strengths and weaknesses.

There are five key ways to learn about your own strengths and non-strengths. These are:

1. Objectively test your abilities using psychological techniques
2. Obtain feedback from your friends, colleagues, bosses and customers

3. Painstakingly examine your biography – track record tells a lot
4. Put yourself in demanding and novel situations which stretch you almost to breaking point, and then learn from your behaviour
5. Use your imagination to explore your latent capacities

All five methods generate valuable, new and different knowledge. Since psychological testing requires professional administration and interpretation, it isn't incorporated in this book. The four remaining methods can be self-managed and we'll start with number two: obtaining feedback from others.

On page 77 you'll find a questionnaire called 'Career Review'. The innocuous title disguises a device for obtaining feedback from others about your achievements. Take a deep breath and make up your mind whether or not you want to gather this information. If you have any doubts, seek advice; don't collect feedback if you feel that you may be damaged by the results. If you decide just to put your toe in the water, try asking one person, whom you know and trust, to complete the Career Review and then discuss the results with you. This will show you the potential value of the questionnaire and help you to assess whether you can cope constructively with the feedback. Then, if you feel comfortable, embark on a larger survey by inviting more people – say, ten – to complete the survey.

Data is evaluated using the Career Review Feedback Interpretation on page 86. The results relate directly to the nine career drivers described in Step Two. You'll begin to see whether your achievements match your career drivers.

Photocopy the questionnaire, write your name in the space provided, and invite people who know you well to complete it. One caution: the Career Review is best suited for those with a track record in work. Students or unemployed people may find that some of the items don't relate to them directly, but they may gain something from collecting the feedback based on their role as a student, trainee or previous job-holder.

Take a deep breath and have a trial run!

CAREER REVIEW

CONFIDENTIAL

This questionnaire is part of a private self-evaluation by

(*name*) ____

who is taking stock of his/her career to date.

You are asked to give feedback on your judgement of this person's current abilities, and agree to a follow-up discussion of the results. Please try to be totally honest and give the best answers you can from your knowledge of the person.

Below you will find forty-five statements. Consider each and assess how far you consider it to be an accurate description of the person at this time. Use the following guidelines for scoring:

The statement is totally true	score 5 points
The statement is largely true	score 4 points
The statement is neither true nor false	score 3 points
The statement is largely untrue	score 2 points
The statement is totally untrue	score 1 point

The Statements

HE/SHE

1. [ ] has demonstrated the capacity to make a significant amount of money

2. ☐ is unusually good at controlling others

3. ☐ has strong personal principles

4. ☐ is recognized as an expert or specialist

5. ☐ is unusually creative

6. ☐ has close social relationships with others at work

7. ☐ is capable of effective self-management

8. ☐ is prudent in making personal decisions

9. ☐ is widely respected by colleagues

10. ☐ has achieved significantly higher income than contemporaries

11. ☐ has found ways to gain power and influence

12. ☐ behaves in a highly principled manner

13. ☐ is regarded as a competent specialist

14. ☐ creates things that no one else has thought of

15. ☐ has warm relationships with others at work

16. ☐ takes independent decisions (i.e. does not look to others)

17. ☐ acts wisely to safeguard future personal prospects

18. ☐ has achieved high social status

19. ☐ negotiates good financial deals for personal reward

20. ☐ succeeds in shaping others' attitudes

21. ☐ produces things which are worthwhile in themselves

22. ☐ maintains a high level of specialized expertise

23. ☐ finds innovative solutions to problems

24. ☐ enjoys close social relationships

25. ☐ has the capacity to be self-reliant

26. ☐ makes career decisions which result in a more secure future

27. ☐ enjoys increasing status and prestige

28. ☐ takes effective steps to maximize personal income

29. ☐ gets into positions which have power and influence

30. ☐ does work which most people consider to be worthwhile

31. ☐ is regularly consulted for specialist knowhow

32. ☐ is recognized as a source of good ideas

33. ☐ gains the affection of others

34. ☐ has the capacity to manage time effectively

35. ☐ has a career which looks secure

36. ☐ is considered to be important by other people

37. ☐ successfully exploits opportunities to increase his/her income

38. ☐ is a competent leader of people

39. ☐ stands firm on matters of principle

40. ☐ keeps up to date as a specialist

41. ☐ exploits unexpected opportunities

42. ☐ has many good friends at work

43. ☐ thrives better when not under the control of others

44. ☐ appears to have long-term security

45. ☐ is considered to be someone who people look up to

That completes the Career Review and thank you for your attention and frankness. Please return the completed questionnaire as soon as possible, taking care to keep the document confidential.

Please enter your name here ______________________________

THANK YOU

Scoring the Career Review Questionnaire

As you collect the completed questionnaires from those who give you feedback, photocopy the scoring grid opposite to provide one blank grid for each respondent. Enter the scores from a completed questionnaire on the scoring grid and total the vertical columns. Then transfer these scores to the summary sheet on the next page.

MR	PI	ME	EX	CR	AF	AU	SE	ST
1	2	3	4	5	6	7	8	9
10	11	12	13	14	15	16	17	18
19	20	21	22	23	24	25	26	27
28	29	30	31	32	33	34	35	36
37	38	39	40	41	42	43	44	45

TOTALS

Career Review Summary Sheet

Enter the scores from each respondent below and then compute average scores by dividing each total by the number of respondents. *Now draw a profile on the next page to help you interpret the results.*

Respondent's Name	MR	PI	ME	EX	CR	AF	AU	SE	ST
1									
2									
3									
4									
5									
6									
7									
8									
9									
10									
TOTALS									
Average									

Career Review Profile

Display the average scores on the chart below and join up the circles to give a diagrammatic profile of the feedback you have been given. Add your own profile from Step Two (page 59) in different coloured ink.

25	25	25	25	25	25	25	25	25
24	24	24	24	24	24	24	24	24
23	23	23	23	23	23	23	23	23
22	22	22	22	22	22	22	22	22
21	21	21	21	21	21	21	21	21
20	20	20	20	20	20	20	20	20
19	19	19	19	19	19	19	19	19
18	18	18	18	18	18	18	18	18
17	17	17	17	17	17	17	17	17
16	16	16	16	16	16	16	16	16
15	15	15	15	15	15	15	15	15
14	14	14	14	14	14	14	14	14
13	13	13	13	13	13	13	13	13
12	12	12	12	12	12	12	12	12
11	11	11	11	11	11	11	11	11
10	10	10	10	10	10	10	10	10
9	9	9	9	9	9	9	9	9
8	8	8	8	8	8	8	8	8
7	7	7	7	7	7	7	7	7
6	6	6	6	6	6	6	6	6
5	5	5	5	5	5	5	5	5
4	4	4	4	4	4	4	4	4
3	3	3	3	3	3	3	3	3
2	2	2	2	2	2	2	2	2
1	1	1	1	1	1	1	1	1
0	0	0	0	0	0	0	0	0
A	**B**	**C**	**D**	**E**	**F**	**G**	**H**	**I**
MATERIAL REWARDS	**POWER/ INFLUENCE**	**MEANING**	**EXPERTISE**	**CREATIVITY**	**AFFILIATION**	**AUTONOMY**	**SECURITY**	**STATUS**

Now read the notes on Interpreting the Career Review Feedback on the next page.

Interpreting the Career Review Feedback

The feedback you have gathered from others on your achievements uses the same nine categories employed in Step Two. Read the brief descriptions below. If you need more information review the detailed explanation of the nine career drivers beginning on page 63.

HIGH SCORE IN MATERIAL REWARDS (MR)
Suggests you are good at exploiting situations to obtain above-average financial rewards and other material benefits. You are well-heeled.

HIGH SCORE IN POWER/INFLUENCE (PI)
Suggests that you are good at getting into situations where you are in charge. You shape the behaviour of others. You are seen as the boss.

HIGH SCORE IN SEARCH FOR MEANING (ME)
Suggests that you are good at identifying your own values and finding work that allows you to express your principles. You are recognized as contributing to improving the quality of life.

HIGH SCORE IN EXPERTISE (EX)
Suggests that you are good at acquiring and maintaining specialized competencies and are seen as a craftsman, technical specialist or expert. You are a practitioner in an acknowledged field of expertise.

HIGH SCORE IN CREATIVITY (CR)
Suggests that you are innovative and capable of devising new or different 'products' which are associated with your name. You are an inventor, problem-solver, constructor or entrepreneur.

HIGH SCORE IN AFFILIATION (AF)
Suggests that you develop positive, supportive and close relationships with others at work. You are socially skilled.

HIGH SCORE IN AUTONOMY (AU)
Suggests that you function well independently of others. You have the capacity and emotional resilience to stand alone. You are able to be your own master.

HIGH SCORE IN SECURITY (SE)
Suggests that you take effective steps to assure your future, and find positions where the risks to your career stability are low. You are a prudent person.

HIGH SCORE IN STATUS (ST)
Suggests that you have the capacity to acquire prestige and social position. Respect, esteem and the regard of others are given to you. You are a person of substance.

Career Review Feedback Analysis

Now you have read the interpretation, look back on the profile on page 85. Lots of provocative questions are bound to emerge. Reflect on the survey by answering the seven questions below and record your notes in the space provided.

1. What patterns can I see in the feedback?

2. How can the patterns be explained?

3. What has surprised me?

4. What has confirmed my views?

5. What questions occur?

6. What are the implications for my job at the moment?

7. What are the implications for my future career?

This will consolidate your thoughts but you still need to learn more about how other people see you. It's time to obtain some direct feedback.

Ask those who completed your Career Reviews to give you time for discussion. Make a point to see those whose opinions you respect and whom you trust to be forthright and objective. Have a long and relaxed discussion on your achievements, using the data from the Career Review as a startpoint. The conversation will be more likely to be productive if you remember to say clearly what you want at the beginning of the conversation and allow plenty of time (up to two hours).

The information you will gain is uniquely valuable for self-development. If you ask people to identify significant experiences in their personal development, the majority reflect for a few moments and then talk about particular comments or conversations which have provided direct and pertinent information about their style. This can profoundly influence the way in which people act.

Feedback, as with many powerful tools, can be abused. Sometimes people have been hurt or deflated through this form of self-learning. It is obviously desirable to find ways of receiving feedback which help you become stronger and more effective, not weaker or inhibited. Feedback enables personal strategies and tactics to be re-evaluated. Acquiring valid and helpful feedback begins with a recognition of its value and a decision to invite it.

The guidelines below help you to receive feedback from others.

PAY ATTENTION. Concentrate on what the person is saying. Demonstrate that you are listening. Give your undivided attention. Absorb what is being said rather than think of implications.

ASK WHAT THE PERSON FEELS. Feelings are as important as thoughts, so need to be made explicit.

SEPARATE DESCRIPTION FROM JUDGEMENT. It is helpful not to ask for judgements about how 'good' or 'bad' you are. Rather ask how the other perceives the situation and make your own evaluation. If you wish to consider opinions then make sure you are separating fact from opinion. Then decide how much value you wish to place on the judgement. Try not to be hurt, or show hurt, when negative points are made.

ASK FOR DIRECTNESS. Good feedback is specific and deals clearly with concrete incidents or particular examples of behaviour. Ask the other person to avoid being vague or unspecific. Try not to defend or justify yourself.

FOCUS ON ACTIONABLE INPUT. It really is not very helpful to receive feedback on things which are outside your control. Useful feedback leads to changes in behaviour.

INVITE COMMENT. To be really useful, feedback has to be wanted. Say what you want and be open to receive truthful comment.

CHECK BACK. Feedback is often tainted by the viewpoint of the giver so check with others to see if there is agreement. Points of difference and similarity can then be clarified so a much more objective view is developed.

We often avoid receiving open feedback but by closing our minds to the observations and thoughts of others we deprive ourselves of information which could be extremely helpful.

Ignoring feedback has serious drawbacks. Individuals benefit from a climate of open and skilful feedback. At the end of your feedback discussion don't forget to thank the other person. Even though you may not like what you have heard, their input will be valuable to you. Discussion provides dispassionate and objective viewpoints on yourself. This is essential. The careerist needs to know how he or she is performing in the real world.

Allow the impact of the feedback to seep into your mind and feelings. When you feel ready, complete the final exercise below and move on to the next step.

Career Review – Closing Stage

From the feedback (both written and verbal) I have learned the following things about myself:

(a)

(b)

(c)

(d)

(e)

(f)

(g)

(h)

(i)

(j)

STEP FOUR

How Satisfied Am I?

'Nothing will come of nothing.'
Shakespeare

YOUR JOB SATISFACTION TODAY

All of us make a living somehow, whether it's as bank managers, shopkeepers, social security claimants, bingo hall ushers, students, librarians, or any one of an almost limitless number of other possibilities. Did you ever see the television programme *What's My Line?* The number of possible jobs is staggering.

With the exception of children, every person has a role which provides the means to keep the wolf from the door. This section furthers your self-study by examining how much satisfaction you are receiving from your role at the present time.

Before we look at your work role it is important to ask, 'What is a job?' In fact, a job is simply a bundle of tasks which someone with power in an organization believes that one person can reliably handle. Most organizations start small. A few pioneers get together to launch a new enterprise. Jobs are flexible and varied. In the early years the work is often precarious but satisfying, as everyone helps each other. However, expansion brings management and co-ordination problems. The organization will disintegrate unless it becomes better administered. The managerial solution is 'specialization' and 'formalization' to better determine who does what. Jobs become narrower and more impersonal. Managers control behaviour by defining job content (e.g. job descriptions), defining what should be done (e.g. procedure manuals), or establishing rules and regulations (e.g. instructions to employees). Rationality and predictability become all-important. The job-holder increasingly becomes a servant of an organizational machine. There are no real options. Organizations must control their employees to survive.

Work can become so highly specialized that the job-holder is virtually imprisoned by the requirements of the task. One of the Richmond Survey respondents, Winston, worked for a time as a packer loading plastic cups into cartons. He described his experience vividly like this: 'This machine that makes the plastic cups spews them out on to a rail. It's my job to pick up the cups and put them in the boxes. The machine clatters like crazy and I have ear-protectors so I'm like a zombie. Sometimes it's weird, like being on dope, and I just ain't really there but my hands are working, sort of. I was doing this thing for about four days when I began to feel this fuzzy stuff growing in my brain. So I tell the man where he can stick his job and that's it.'

Of course, this is an extreme example. Many jobs offer more than Winston's packing role in the plastic cup factory, but all jobs limit the holders. The structure of tasks in a work role shapes experience. We call a mismatch between what the person wants and what the job offers 'job dissatisfaction'.

There's no such thing as a job which is intrinsically satisfying or unsatisfying. Almost any job you could think of is hated by some people and greatly enjoyed by others. Job satisfaction is the outcome of a good fit betwen a person's career drivers and the benefits that he or she gains from doing the job.

It's important for careerists to review their current job carefully in order to discover whether it gives satisfaction and provides development opportunities. Before we get started, note that a useful distinction can be drawn between satisfaction with a job and satisfaction in a job (see W. W. Daniel, 'Industrial Behaviour and Orientation to Work: a Critique', *Journal of Applied Management Studies,* vol. 6, October 1969, pp. 366–75). This was clearly illustrated by Harold, who had once worked as a machinist. He said: 'I was basically pleased to have the job. There was nothing really wrong with it, except that the job had absolutely no scope for individuality. A trained monkey could do it – only the monkey would have got bored to death.'

Jobs have a great effect on the holder. From one viewpoint they are time-consuming and confining. Each morning for perhaps fifty years your postman rises early and carries letters from door to door. He structures his whole life around his postal duties. Jobs are a ball and chain which limit the holder to a specified range of behaviour.

The potential for satisfaction is, to a certain extent, built into the structure of a job. A supermarket cashier, for example, spends seven hours every day sitting at a checkout till, punching in numbers. Although the job brings contact with many people, it has no room for the expression of any creativity or individuality.

People have to look at the confines of potential jobs very carefully in order to see whether they offer the possibility of satisfaction. When people fail to do this, things go wrong. Richard, now a priest, began his career as a draughtsman. He said: 'I spent my days standing at a drawing board planning how mouldings should be manufactured. As time went on, the job seemed to be more and more meaningless and isolated to me. My vitality was in my life outside work, since I was involved in the church, the community and so on. Eventually I took the plunge and became a student of divinity. Looking back, I realize now that draughtsmanship would have killed the most precious parts of me.'

Richard's story is extreme but not untypical. Almost all (91 per cent) of the respondents in the Richmond Study were unsatisfied with some aspects of their jobs. It soon became clear that major dissatisfactions were related to job demands which ran counter to the person's current career drivers.

Fortunately, the picture is not as bleak as it first appears. Jobs have another dimension – they also liberate. One way to understand the liberating quality of work is to examine what happens to people who do not have a job.

The absence of a job is felt as a profound loss. People march in thousands to protest against unemployment. All manner of social malaises are blamed on inadequate job opportunities. Certainly, men and women who lose their jobs are more prone to illness, depression and suicide. Many people are prepared to sacrifice their health and family life for job success.

Katherine, a marketing executive, waxed lyrical about the significance of work. She said, 'My job is totally essential to me. It brings me into intimate contact with all parts of society, organizes my life, satisfies basic needs and gives an awfully warm feeling of contributing.' The Richmond Survey, like many other occupational studies, demonstrated that work plays a vital role in society. It binds the individual into the 'real world', and provides legitimate opportunities to relate to others. The accomplishment of difficult or challenging tasks is intrinsically satisfying. Social status and prestige are closely associated with occupations.

The structure of work is not static. Jobs change their form with technological advance. Our forefathers' employment opportunities were very different from our own. One of my grandfathers was a basket maker whilst another was a hansom cab driver. Neither job exists in the same form today. Carefully reviewing career histories of Richmond Survey respondents enabled broad trends to be identified. These were:

- Traditional crafts and skills have largely gone
- There is an enormous emphasis on efficiency
- Greater use of mechanical and intelligent machines reduces the opportunity for low-grade careers
- There is a need for high-grade skills in designing and caring for systems
- Fundamental changes in employment are occurring
- Careerists need to undertake frequent retraining
- Careerists are required to accept significant increases in geographical mobility
- Some people demonstrate considerable social mobility
- There is more dependence on personal achievement (less emphasis on the extended family)
- There is a higher level of general education
- There are higher demands on the individual to perform well

How Satisfied Am I?

Work roles are obviously shaped by such general trends but careerists are more immediately influenced by their job history. An important 'payoff cycle' can be identified. Positive elements of a new job often become negative in time. It may seem remarkable that a job, once full of interest and excitement, can become unadulterated drudgery. But this is the truth. In fact, four stages can be identified:

Stage One: Demand and Learning

The new job-holder is required to learn. Co-workers have to be understood, relationships established, situations appraised, knowledge built and skills acquired. Petra described her new job as personnel manager as a 'culture shock'. She said, 'Really, I wasn't sure I could cope. Everything was coming at once. There was something new every second. I'm working sixty hours a week. I even finished a paper on Christmas Day. I've never been so stretched.' Demanding jobs are full of learning opportunities.

Stage Two: Growth to Conscious Competence

As the first weeks and months pass the job-holder becomes more experienced and begins to settle in. Ways to be efficient and effective are found. Relationships are built and skills developed. Both the formal and informal systems begin to be understood. Arthur gave an illustration. He said, 'I feel that I am getting on top of the job after four months. I know what's important and who's important. It's starting to get organized.' The growth stage is fulfilling and also developmental. Competence is slowly developed and new capability acquired.

Stage Three: Mastery

After a significant length of time the job-holder becomes master of the role. Most issues have been successfully handled in the past. Chris, a prison officer, said, 'I really know this job. I feel totally confident. It's not easy, but well within my ability.' The mastery stage still has potential for personal growth. However, the level of challenge usually reduces and so the seeds of the fourth stage begin to germinate.

Stage Four: Ease or Decline

After an enjoyable period of mastery, all becomes routine and the person copes with challenges with a practised competence. There are few new growth opportunities. Surplus energy may go into hobbies, job expansion, or sourness. Mike had been a pilot for eleven years and was clearly in this fourth stage. He said, 'It's all routine to me now. Almost all the time I operate within my competence. I could do it in my sleep. The company couldn't give a damn. They just want their 747s running to schedule and they pay us so much that we are stuck in a mink-lined trap.' This is a dangerous phase for upwardly mobile careerists who cannot afford to lose momentum and shrink. Not only does their career suffer but they also lose a driving and acquisitive personal orientation.

Satisfaction with work is not only gained by having a job. Many people undertake quasi-work assignments on a voluntary basis. This is especially true in the fourth stage of job progression. Although unrewarded financially, voluntary roles are almost indistinguishable from ordinary jobs. Petra, a personnel manager, wrote short stories in her spare time, and Arthur, an electronics engineer, ran a smallholding with pigs, chickens, vegetable crops and so on. People find ways of fulfilling their drivers outside the rather haphazard job market. They use their initiative to fill the gaps.

In the practical work for this section we focus on your job. The purpose is to explore whether your current job is capable of giving you the psychological payoffs that you want. A simple analogy makes the point. Let's assume that a job gives you nourishment like food in a restaurant. The question is: 'Are you eating in the right place?' A restaurant that only serves steaks is anathema to a vegetarian and one that only serves fried foods is unhealthy for almost everyone. The aim is to find a restaurant which suits you.

On the next page you find the Job Satisfaction Survey. This will help you get started. Complete the survey as suggested, and then progress with your job study.

What if you don't have a job at the moment? Some people undertaking this career review will be mature students or, as actors say, 'resting' between jobs. Whether you are currently employed or not you will find it helpful to use the Job Satisfaction Survey to evaluate your current, or most recent, job. This will help you to understand your experience better and, more importantly, it provides you with a tool which enables you to consider any job that might be offered to you in the future.

JOB SATISFACTION SURVEY

The survey helps clarify the extent to which your job provides satisfaction. This is an assessment of a role, *not* of you as a person. Think about the requirements of your job as objectively as you can, drawing on your own experience of it. Define your work role in the space below.

My work role is ______________________________

Look at each of the forty-five statements strictly in relation to this role and allocate points as follows:

Entirely and always true	5 points
Largely true	4 points
Sometimes true	3 points
Largely untrue	2 points
Totally untrue	1 point
Not relevant	0 points

Write your score in the space provided next to each statement. Do not look at the explanation of results until you have answered the questions. Work quite quickly – your first reactions are wanted. Do not look back at previous answers: consider each item afresh. The questionnaire takes about fifteen minutes to complete.

The Statements (score each item *only* in relation to the role defined above)

1. ☐ The material benefits are high
2. ☐ This role gives substantial control over people
3. ☐ What is produced is worthwhile
4. ☐ Specialized abilities are essential to perform the job
5. ☐ A creative approach to problem-solving is essential
6. ☐ There is the opportunity for good social relationships with others
7. ☐ The key decisions about how work is done are made by the job-holder
8. ☐ This role has long-term security
9. ☐ The role gives high status in the wider community
10. ☐ The role provides ample material rewards
11. ☐ The job-holder controls how significant resources will be allocated

12. ☐ What is produced has real importance to others

13. ☐ Special skills are essential to perform the role

14. ☐ The job requires substantial creativity

15. ☐ There is ample opportunity to develop good relationships with co-workers

16. ☐ The job-holder has a high degree of freedom from organizational constraints

17. ☐ The role is considered permanent

18. ☐ This role gives high prestige to the holder

19. ☐ Material rewards are high

20. ☐ The role gives substantial influence over others

21. ☐ What is produced benefits people

22. ☐ This role requires someone with a high level of specialized expertise

23. ☐ New solutions to problems often have to be found

24. [ ] There is the opportunity to build close personal relationships

25. [ ] The job-holder decides what is important or unimportant

26. [ ] Performing the role brings job security

27. [ ] The role gives high social standing in the community at large

28. [ ] High material rewards go with the job

29. [ ] There is significant power to decide what should be done

30. [ ] What is produced is important in itself

31. [ ] This role requires specialized expertise for adequate performance

32. [ ] New ways of doing things are often needed

33. [ ] There are frequent opportunities to meet and talk to interesting people

34. [ ] The job-holder sets his or her own priorities

35. [ ] This role is generally considered to give long-term security

36. ☐ The role is considered prestigious

37. ☐ Material rewards are considered more than reasonable

38. ☐ The job-holder takes decisions about what other people should do

39. ☐ The actual output is considered worthwhile in itself

40. ☐ Specialized abilities are required to perform the job adequately

41. ☐ There are opportunities to do things which are totally new

42. ☐ There is a lot of encouragement and support from others

43. ☐ The job-holder takes the important decisions about what is going to be done

44. ☐ The role gives a high level of personal security

45. ☐ This role carries with it a high level of social status

Job Satisfaction Survey Scoring Grid

Copy your scores from the questionnaire on to the grid below. Then add up the scores in each vertical column and write the totals in the boxes provided. When you have done this, copy the results on to the profile on the next page.

1	2	3	4	5	6	7	8	9
10	11	12	13	14	15	16	17	18
19	20	21	22	23	24	25	26	27
28	29	30	31	32	33	34	35	36
37	38	39	40	41	42	43	44	45

TOTALS

A	B	C	D	E	F	G	H	I

Job Satisfaction Profile

Display your scores on the chart below by circling the numbers you scored and joining up the circles to give a diagrammatic profile of the potential satisfaction from your job.

25	25	25	25	25	25	25	25	25
24	24	24	24	24	24	24	24	24
23	23	23	23	23	23	23	23	23
22	22	22	22	22	22	22	22	22
21	21	21	21	21	21	21	21	21
20	20	20	20	20	20	20	20	20
19	19	19	19	19	19	19	19	19
18	18	18	18	18	18	18	18	18
17	17	17	17	17	17	17	17	17
16	16	16	16	16	16	16	16	16
15	15	15	15	15	15	15	15	15
14	14	14	14	14	14	14	14	14
13	13	13	13	13	13	13	13	13
12	12	12	12	12	12	12	12	12
11	11	11	11	11	11	11	11	11
10	10	10	10	10	10	10	10	10
9	9	9	9	9	9	9	9	9
8	8	8	8	8	8	8	8	8
7	7	7	7	7	7	7	7	7
6	6	6	6	6	6	6	6	6
5	5	5	5	5	5	5	5	5
4	4	4	4	4	4	4	4	4
3	3	3	3	3	3	3	3	3
2	2	2	2	2	2	2	2	2
1	1	1	1	1	1	1	1	1
0	0	0	0	0	0	0	0	0
A	**B**	**C**	**D**	**E**	**F**	**G**	**H**	**I**
MATERIAL REWARDS	**POWER/ INFLUENCE**	**MEANING**	**EXPERTISE**	**CREATIVITY**	**AFFILIATION**	**AUTONOMY**	**SECURITY**	**STATUS**

Now complete the assessment of results on the next page.

Job Satisfaction Survey: Assessment of Results

The nine career drivers are reviewed briefly below and there is a space beside each paragraph to enter your scores from page 106 so that you can assess whether your present role is capable of meeting your personal needs and wants. The maximum score is 25 and the minimum is 0. A high score suggests that the role has the potential to provide you with a high level of satisfaction. A low score means the opposite.

A ☐ MATERIAL REWARDS: The role provides opportunities to acquire tangible rewards, often financial, which enable an above-average standard of living to be maintained.

B ☐ POWER/INFLUENCE: The role provides opportunities to influence and control people, direct the use of resources and shape events.

C ☐ MEANING: The role provides opportunities to produce products which are considered inherently worthwhile.

D ☐ EXPERTISE: The role uses specialized knowledge, ability, skills and training.

E ☐ CREATIVITY: The role provides opportunities to express creative potential and has capacity for innovation. It fulfils the wish to be identified with new enterprise.

F ☐ AFFILIATION: The role provides opportunities to build fulfilling human relationships and meet social needs.

G ☐ AUTONOMY: The role provides opportunities to set priorities and make decisions for oneself.

H ☐ SECURITY: The role provides opportunities to predict the future and gives stability.

I ☐ STATUS: The role provides opportunities to acquire social esteem in the community at large.

You have now completed the Job Satisfaction Survey for your work role. Enter your scores on the profile on page 85.

MID-POINT REVIEW

Mark the scores from Step Two (page 59), Three (page 84) and Four (page 107) on the table on the next page, then calculate your frustration factors (the degree to which your current work role is not meeting your needs) and performance gaps (where you are not achieving what you are driven towards).

High scores (more than plus 5) in column C suggest that a career driver is not being fulfilled by your current role.

High scores (more than plus 5) on column E suggest that your present performance does not allow your career driver to be exploited.

When you have completed the analysis it is time for reflection. Look at the results and ask what they mean to you. Does the pattern surprise you or does it confirm your preconceptions? It often helps to talk to a friend before proceeding further.

Career Drivers Analysis

	A	B	C	D	E
	WHAT I WANT AND NEED Scores from page 59	WHAT MY JOB GIVES ME Scores from page 107	FRUSTRATION FACTOR (Subtract column B from column A)	ACHIEVEMENTS Scores from page 84	PERFORMANCE GAP (Subtract column D from column A)
MATERIAL REWARDS					
POWER/ INFLUENCE					
MEANING					
EXPERTISE					
CREATIVITY					
AFFILIATION					
AUTONOMY					
SECURITY					
STATUS					

Complete your mid-point review by answering the questions on the next page.

Concluding the Mid-point Career Drivers Review

You are getting to grips with career drivers and it is helpful to add a historical perspective. Answer the questions below, then look over your answers to identify what drivers were current for you at different stages of your life.

1. What were your best and worst subjects at school?

2. What made you choose your specializations during your later years of education?

3. When you were a child, what occupations did you consider for an adult career?

4. What did your parents (and other older people) encourage you to study?

5. What really interested you as a student?

6. What voluntary activities interested you whilst studying?

7. Looking back over your student days what would you wish to do differently?

8. Why did you choose your first job?

9. Think about all your job changes: what were the reasons for your choices?

Job Change	*Reason*

10. What assignments or tasks have you performed really well at work?

Assignment	*How was excellence measured?*

11. What assignments or tasks have you performed to an unacceptable standard?

Assignment	*How was substandard performance measured?*

12. Look back over your career to date: what have been the achievements which meant most to you?

Achievement	*Why especially important?*

13. What are your current hobbies?

14. What has felt wrong in your career to date?

What has felt wrong?	*Why?*

15. How do you describe your trade or profession to others?

That concludes the mid-point review. Look back over your answers and spend some time reflecting before you proceed further.

STEP FIVE

What Are My Talents?

'Genius does what it must, and Talent does what it can.'
Owen Meredith

TALENTS

Some months after I interviewed Mark he asked for a meeting to discuss a very unusual and interesting career choice. Mark was a scientist who worked in the research laboratories of a major company. He also had a gift for music and played an electronic trumpet (no, I hadn't heard of it either!). One day, six lads from the Midlands Rock and Roll Band invited him to sit in. They liked his music and style and soon he became a regular member. The band was playing to increasingly packed audiences and the lads were offered a chance of lifetime – a tour of the Far East, Australia and New Zealand. The band wanted Mark to join them. His question was: 'Should I go?'

Mark had two different sorts of talents. First, he was an insightful and methodical scientist, and secondly, he was a brilliant musician. His dilemma was: 'Which talent should I exploit, and what will be the impact on my lifestyle?' After much inner doubt Mark decided to take a year's leave of absence and become a pop star for a while.

Mark was engaged in a search. He wanted to discover what he had to give to the world, in other words Mark was searching to define his talents. Since careers are avenues for the expression of talents, it is necessary to learn how to identify and categorize talents in ways which will be useful to us.

Talents are powers or abilities intrinsic in a person. It's

impossible to manufacture talents, although they can be developed through education and experience. The notion of a talent is useful, since it suggests that there is latent potential which is seeking an outlet. The careerist's task is to discover his or her own particular talents and exploit them to the full.

Not everyone can do everything. Talents, like big feet or blond hair, are usually determined by the time we reach adulthood. There is persuasive evidence that talent is largely given or acquired through very early learning. By the time someone is old enough to read this book, the basic dimensions of talent are firmly established. This is not to say that we cannot evolve further. New competencies are acquired throughout life, and attitudes and values change with experience, but the foundations of our special contribution to life are already firmly laid.

Talents provide the means to satisfy career drivers. For example, a man driven to seek material rewards can become a millionaire by playing snooker, building houses or opening a factory, but not by being a police officer or sweeping the streets. Individuals want to satisfy their drivers but the world wants jobs to be done. Talents are the reason why someone will pay for your services. They are your gifts: an interface between you and the world.

It's difficult, perhaps even impossible, to measure talents, especially those which are latent! You'd need a clairvoyant, not a psychologist. In this section talent is taken to mean possessing a native capacity which enables the person to rapidly acquire the competence to perform to a high standard. In other words, a talent is a predisposition to perform well.

Ruth, the actress, expressed the notion of talent very well. She said: 'I've been performing ever since I can remember. When I was about three I used to run round in circles, show my knickers, and do impressions of dogs or the fishmonger. I liked approval. My parents sent me to ballet classes and elocution lessons and I really took to it. My wall was covered with certificates. I liked performing, it came fairly easily and I did it well. Wasn't I a clever girl!'

Talent is different from strength in that a strength is an existing resource, whereas a talent may be latent or underdeveloped.

Caroline was a housewife who discovered by accident that she had a talent for interior design. Now she employs four people, has a professional nanny to look after the children and has recently bought a holiday house on the island of Mustique. If she hadn't chanced to meet a neighbour's aunt, a successful textile designer, Caroline's artistic and business abilities might well have lain fallow for life. Exploiting talents requires experiment, not just reflection. Caroline said: 'I wouldn't have discovered that I had an eye for interior design without an enforced break from a demanding lifestyle.'

Careful analysis of the Richmond Survey results enabled us to observe that almost everyone's talents were only partly expressed. They were subject to many constraints through environment. For example, social class, racial origin and family upbringing played major roles. Talents often lay dormant, or were only apparent through hobbies.

There appear to be inherent satisfactions in simply expressing talents. Those who were mathematically inclined got pleasure from solving puzzles, while artistic people found equal joy in painting, sculpting, writing and so on. Career satisfaction was linked, at least in the minds of careerists, with the extent to which their talents were exploited by work opportunities. Harold made this point clearly when he said: 'I think of a person as being like an animal. A tiger is born to be bold and wild. If you confine it in a zoo, it can't be its true self. There is an urge for self-expression which is very powerful. One has to be who one is.'

For careerists, the task of identifying talents is especially important. In its Biblical sense the word 'talent' means currency. Personal talents are coinage in your purse. They are what attracts the world to your door. It's crucial to identify, develop and exploit your own talents and to transform them into marketable competencies.

After considerable analysis of Richmond Survey interview transcripts I found that it was useful to categorize talents into seven groups or clusters. These include all the common talents, but omit some rarer capabilities. Chris, for example, is a dog handler in a high-security prison, but keeps snakes as a hobby. Tim, while working overseas as a doctor, became interested in hunting with falcons. Neither snake-charming nor falconry fitted into common talent clusters!

The Talents Audit beginning on page 121 starts you thinking about your talents analytically. There are no right or wrong answers. A study of the relationship between scores provides the most useful outcome. Some people mark themselves harder than others, so be suspicious of comparisons between people. Nevertheless, the Talents Audit has proved an important stage in identifying what attributes people offer to the world.

The procedure for using the Talents Audit is:

1. Complete the Talents Audit yourself (it takes about half an hour). Take care to be as objective and honest as you can
2. Record your Talents Audit Profile (page 132)
3. Discuss the results with at least three friends or colleagues who know you very well
4. Complete the Talent Summary (page 138)

TALENTS AUDIT

This audit helps you to assess your talents and then group them into useful clusters.

There are seven sections. Each considers a particular cluster of talents which you may or may not possess. Both work and non-work experiences should be taken into account. Answer all twelve questions in each section by thinking about people of approximately the same age as yourself and comparing yourself with them. Use the following system for scoring.

e	d	c	b	a

0% 10% 20% 30% 40% 50% 60% 70% 80% 90% 100%

Low compared with others — **High compared with others**

Talents Audit Section A

1. I am very knowledgeable in at least one aspect of the arts — e d c b a

2. I fully express my individuality in the way I behave — e d c b a

3.	I have the ability to write with great imagination	e	d	c	b	a
4.	I have the ability to write well-constructed essays	e	d	c	b	a
5.	Other people are impressed by me in conversation	e	d	c	b	a
6.	I can hold the rapt attention of large audiences	e	d	c	b	a
7.	Sometimes I strongly confront the values people use to guide their lives	e	d	c	b	a
8.	I take great care in the ways I present myself to others	e	d	c	b	a
9.	I play a musical instrument to professional standards	e	d	c	b	a
10.	I am a good performer of at least one of the dramatic arts	e	d	c	b	a
11.	I am able to tolerate a high degree of uncertainty	e	d	c	b	a
12.	I learn from looking deeply into myself	e	d	c	b	a

SCORING
Add up the total number of 'a' scores _____ multiply by 5 =
Add up the total number of 'b' scores _____ multiply by 4 =
Add up the total number of 'c' scores _____ multiply by 3 =
Add up the total number of 'd' scores _____ multiply by 2 =
Add up the total number of 'e' scores _____ multiply by 1 =

TOTAL = 12 **A** TOTAL =

Talents Audit Section B

		e	d	c	b	a
1.	I am very knowledgeable in one 'people-orientated' academic discipline	e	d	c	b	a
2.	I am very active in helping others	e	d	c	b	a
3.	I am sensitive to the needs of others	e	d	c	b	a
4.	I am a good listener	e	d	c	b	a
5.	I genuinely respect individual differences between people	e	d	c	b	a
6.	I build relationships of trust with other people	e	d	c	b	a
7.	I relate warmly to other people	e	d	c	b	a
8.	I take great care to put myself in the other person's shoes	e	d	c	b	a
9.	I work well in teams	e	d	c	b	a
10.	I am an effective teacher	e	d	c	b	a
11.	I am a skilled counsellor	e	d	c	b	a
12.	I am a skilled helper of others (any expertise)	e	d	c	b	a

SCORING

Add up the total number of 'a' scores _____ multiply by 5 =
Add up the total number of 'b' scores _____ multiply by 4 =
Add up the total number of 'c' scores _____ multiply by 3 =
Add up the total number of 'd' scores _____ multiply by 2 =
Add up the total number of 'e' scores _____ multiply by 1 =

TOTAL = 12 **B** TOTAL =

Talents Audit Section C

1. I am very capable in a craft or technical skill (any)	e	d	c	b	a
2. I find effective solutions to practical problems	e	d	c	b	a
3. I am very knowledgeable about certain products or processes (any)	e	d	c	b	a
4. I have a real aptitude for finding mechanical faults	e	d	c	b	a
5. I have a real aptitude for finding electronic faults	e	d	c	b	a
6. I build complex things well (constructions or products)	e	d	c	b	a
7. I repair complex things well (constructions or products)	e	d	c	b	a
8. I am patient when faced with technical problems	e	d	c	b	a
9. I use tools skilfully	e	d	c	b	a
10. I am good with my hands	e	d	c	b	a
11. I am able to discover the principles of how things work	e	d	c	b	a
12. I work well with natural materials (wood, clay etc.)	e	d	c	b	a

SCORING
Add up the total number of 'a' scores _____ multiply by 5 =
Add up the total number of 'b' scores _____ multiply by 4 =
Add up the total number of 'c' scores _____ multiply by 3 =
Add up the total number of 'd' scores _____ multiply by 2 =
Add up the total number of 'e' scores _____ multiply by 1 =

TOTAL = 12 **C** TOTAL =

Talents Audit Section D

1. I cope well with mathematical or statistical challenges	e	d	c	b	a
2. I rapidly appreciate technically complex problems	e	d	c	b	a
3. I approach tasks using disciplined scientific methods	e	d	c	b	a
4. I insist that people show that their conclusions are based on demonstrable facts	e	d	c	b	a
5. I study situations very carefully before coming to conclusions	e	d	c	b	a
6. I plan technical projects effectively	e	d	c	b	a
7. I rationally assess the strengths and weaknesses of arguments	e	d	c	b	a

8. I am comfortable using computers and other data-processing devices — e d c b a

9. I rigorously question conventional answers to problems — e d c b a

10. I conduct experiments rather than assume that I know the answer — e d c b a

11. I often read scientific/technical journals for pleasure (often = one per week) — e d c b a

12. I keep up to date with technical developments in my field — e d c b a

SCORING

Add up the total number of 'a' scores _____ multiply by 5 =
Add up the total number of 'b' scores _____ multiply by 4 =
Add up the total number of 'c' scores _____ multiply by 3 =
Add up the total number of 'd' scores _____ multiply by 2 =
Add up the total number of 'e' scores _____ multiply by 1 =

TOTAL = 12 **D** TOTAL =

Talents Audit Section E

1. I have been considered to be a successful manager at senior level — e d c b a

2. I adopt a highly organized approach to my use of time — e d c b a

3. I take strong initiatives to assist people to perform more effectively	e	d	c	b	a
4. I systematically analyse the effectiveness of organizations	e	d	c	b	a
5. I am acknowledged as a competent leader	e	d	c	b	a
6. I identify and exploit the talents of other people	e	d	c	b	a
7. I invest considerable energy in setting objectives	e	d	c	b	a
8. I efficiently organize my desk/office	e	d	c	b	a
9. I carefully monitor the performance of others	e	d	c	b	a
10. I keep up to date with at least one aspect of management science	e	d	c	b	a
11. I read management journals and books often (often = one per week)	e	d	c	b	a
12. I present well-argued cases to acquire resources for my projects	e	d	c	b	a

SCORING

Add up the total number of 'a' scores _____ multiply by 5 =
Add up the total number of 'b' scores _____ multiply by 4 =
Add up the total number of 'c' scores _____ multiply by 3 =
Add up the total number of 'd' scores _____ multiply by 2 =
Add up the total number of 'e' scores _____ multiply by 1 =

TOTAL = 12 **E** TOTAL =

Talents Audit Section F

1. I am a teacher/instructor of a physical sport (any)	e	d	c	b	a
2. I have considerable physical agility	e	d	c	b	a
3. I am a competent sportsman or sportswoman (high = county standard)	e	d	c	b	a
4. I am very confident in outdoor environments	e	d	c	b	a
5. I have performed as an athlete in front of a crowd/audience (high = county standard)	e	d	c	b	a
6. I am physically very strong	e	d	c	b	a
7. I am physically fit at the present time (high = could run 10 km in 40 minutes or equivalent)	e	d	c	b	a
8. I volunteer to enter demanding physical situations or environments (high = mountain climbing or caving expeditions or similar)	e	d	c	b	a
9. I adapt well to unexpected and arduous physical demands	e	d	c	b	a
10. I methodically assess physical risks before committing myself to an arduous project	e	d	c	b	a
11. I undertake a disciplined training regime to develop physical skills	e	d	c	b	a

12. I continue to be largely effective despite bodily tiredness — e d c b a

SCORING

Add up the total number of 'a' scores_____ multiply by 5 =
Add up the total number of 'b' scores_____ multiply by 4 =
Add up the total number of 'c' scores_____ multiply by 3 =
Add up the total number of 'd' scores_____ multiply by 2 =
Add up the total number of 'e' scores_____ multiply by 1 =

TOTAL = 12 **F** TOTAL =

Talents Audit Section G

1. I influence other people to change their behaviour considerably (high = many people) — e d c b a

2. I am very confident when putting across my case — e d c b a

3. I often win arguments — e d c b a

4. I have clear views about what should be done — e d c b a

5. I often get into positions where people look to me for decisions — e d c b a

6. I successfully 'sell' things to people (high = many people) — e d c b a

	e	d	c	b	a
7. I am sensitive to what other people want to hear	e	d	c	b	a
8. I open people's minds to different ways of thinking (high = many people)	e	d	c	b	a
9. I considerably change my approach to others depending on their character	e	d	c	b	a
10. I have a very wide circle of contacts	e	d	c	b	a
11. I get superior treatment wherever I go	e	d	c	b	a
12. I rapidly master new situations	e	d	c	b	a

SCORING
Add up the total number of 'a' scores ____ multiply by 5 =
Add up the total number of 'b' scores ____ multiply by 4 =
Add up the total number of 'c' scores ____ multiply by 3 =
Add up the total number of 'd' scores ____ multiply by 2 =
Add up the total number of 'e' scores ____ multiply by 1 =

TOTAL = 12 **G** TOTAL =

Talents Audit: Interpreting the Results

You've just completed the Talents Audit and now you're probably wondering what it all means. The audit is structured to give you feedback on seven common talent clusters. These are:

(A) SELF-EXPRESSION
(B) CARING/HELPING
(C) WORKING WITH THINGS
(D) APPLIED SCIENCE
(E) ADMINISTRATION/MANAGEMENT
(F) PHYSICAL PROWESS
(G) INFLUENCE/PERSUASION

Your scores for each are not significant in themselves, but the comparative relationship between scores for the seven clusters is very interesting. This helps you identify the 'gifts' that you contribute to the world of work.

You should now complete the profile on the next page.

Talents Audit Profile

Copy the total scores from each Talents Audit section into the box below.

	Points Total
(A) SELF-EXPRESSION	
(B) CARING/HELPING	
(C) WORKING WITH THINGS	
(D) APPLIED SCIENCE	
(E) ADMINISTRATION/ MANAGEMENT	
(F) PHYSICAL PROWESS	
(G) INFLUENCE/PERSUASION	

The next section gives a detailed explanation of these talent clusters.

TALENT CLUSTERS

To understand what is distinctive about each of the seven clusters read this section and then complete the suggested Talent Summary on page 138.

CLUSTER 'A' – SELF-EXPRESSION

People high in self-expression have artistic, creative and expressive talents. They exploit inner intellectual, emotional and physical resources in ways which others appreciate.

Talents of this kind are expressed through one or more of the following vehicles: writing, speaking, drama, film, music, dance, painting, drawing, sculpting, pottery and so on. A person may develop craft or other skills in order to serve their talent for self-expression.

Self-expression has its source within people who may feel that they have important messages, a wish to make a contribution to others, or simply a desire to share their inner experiences with others.

Those with very high self-expression talents are innovative in the arts and cultural life. They are the famous actors, authors, painters and sculptors whose lifestyle is devoted to their art.

CLUSTER 'B' – CARING/HELPING

Those high in caring/helping are committed to improving the quality of other people's lives. They form positive relationships and perform services for their fellows.

These talents are expressed through one or more of the following vehicles: medicine, education, religion, social work, counselling, child-care, recreation, training and so on. Caring/helping can also be expressed with animals and natural environments. The person with caring/helping talents may develop administration/

management skills, but only in order to improve their ability to help or care for others.

Caring/helping has its source in the individual's belief in the importance of community. But it isn't necessarily a soft or compliant stance. People of this type can be demanding and authoritative.

Those with very high caring and helping talents are the great educators, healers, and helpers of others.

CLUSTER 'C' – WORKING WITH THINGS

Those high in working with things are accomplished manufacturers, designers, repairers, and maintainers. They are practical and prefer concrete tasks. Talents like this are expressed through one or more of these vehicles: craftsmanship, product knowledge, mechanical or electronic knowhow, maintenance technology, manual or diagnostic skills. Some people may develop their administrative/management skills in order to work with things. Technological expertise may be acquired in order to solve practical problems.

Working with things has its source within the person's respect for the works of man. People in this category enjoy products for their own sake; this appreciation may be inspired by elegance, fitness for purpose, style, form, intricacy or complexity.

Those with very high talents in working with things are great inventors, designers, constructors of artefacts, and craftsmen or women.

CLUSTER 'D' – APPLIED SCIENCE

Those high in applied science have an established body of knowledge and methodology which they apply in order to perform specialized services. They provide solutions to scientific or technological problems, and they cope with complex information-handling and decision-making.

Talents of this sort are expressed through one or more of these vehicles: physical sciences, technology, engineering, architecture, social sciences, mathematics, and other technical disciplines. A person may develop skills in management to assist them in solving large or complex problems.

Applied science has its source within the person's love of rational enquiry. People like this use methodologies based on valid and repeatable experimentation. Their talents are in acquiring technical knowhow, then utilizing and creatively adapting it to specific applications.

People who are very high in applied science are great engineers, scientists, inventors and technological innovators.

CLUSTER 'E' – ADMINISTRATION/MANAGEMENT

People high in administration/management possess the talents to organize and co-ordinate resources in order to achieve specific objectives. They are skilled in the identification and exploitation of potential capability and maintenance of man/machine systems.

Talents like these are expressed through one or more of the following vehicles: management, supervision, entrepreneurship, administrative systems design, consultancy, ownership of business, politics, and senior roles in hierarchies. Such people may develop other talents such as influence/persuasion in order to administer/ manage successfully.

Administration/management has its origin in respect for order and control. Talents are expressed by setting goals, communicating purpose, monitoring performance, planning and co-ordination.

Those with very high administration/management talents are great industrialists, bureaucrats, organizers and generals.

CLUSTER 'F' – PHYSICAL PROWESS

People who are high in physical prowess have athletic, kinaesthetic, muscular, manual and endurance skills. They exploit the potential of the body.

This kind of talent is expressed through one or more of these vehicles: using physical strength, using athletic ability, manual occupations, adventurous pursuits, rural occupations, physically demanding roles. People may develop other skills, for example in caring and helping, in order to make a living out of their prowess.

Physical prowess, as the term suggests, has its origin in the love of physical expression. It is associated with enjoyment of movement, activity and the environment.

Those with very high physical prowess talents are great athletes, sports players, adventurers and soldiers. In post-industrial society many physical occupations have been mechanized, so this talent cluster is often expressed through recreation and games.

CLUSTER 'G' – INFLUENCE/PERSUASION

People high in influence/persuasion have talents for getting others to agree with their views or buy their products. They are able to charm, impress, argue, cajole, beguile, coax, decoy, lure, and generally get their own way.

Talents in this category are expressed by one or more of these vehicles: public relations, selling, marketing, advising, community leadership, and staff roles in organizations. People may develop other skills, for example in administration/management.

Influence/persuasion has its source in the desire to have power over other people and to manipulate their thoughts and feelings. It is a talent associated with productive social relationships.

Those with very high talents in influence/persuasion are great intellectual and moral leaders, marketeers, advocates of causes and sales people.

CONCLUSION TO STEP FIVE

These are the seven talent clusters. Each is an inextricably tangled combination of attitudes, inherited attributes, physical gifts, learned skills and adult dispositions. Carccrists can exploit them, and should work hard in order fully to realize their talent repertoires.

In order to consolidate your insight into your own talents, find three or more people who know you well and arrange to have a conversation with them. Use the guidelines in Step Three beginning on page 90 to help you get the most out of the meeting. Show them the results of your Talents Audit (page 132) and invite them to comment on each specific item. Ask for concrete examples of how you demonstrate talents in your everyday working life. When you have completed these conversations fill in the Talent Summary overleaf. You are then ready to move on to Step Six.

TALENTS SUMMARY

Reflect on the results of the Talents Audit and the subsequent conversations and answer this brief questionnaire.

1. I believe my primary talent is . . .

2. I am also talented in . . .

3. My talents have been developed (*tick as appropriate*)
   (a) Totally (i.e. no room for improvement)
   (b) Largely
   (c) To some extent
   (d) A small amount
   (e) Not at all

4. The talent I should most enjoy developing is . . .

5. The talent it would be most 'beneficial' to develop is . . .

6. In the past three years I have developed my talents in the following ways . . .

STEP SIX

What Constrains Me?

'Man was born free, and everywhere he is in chains.'
Rousseau

CONSTRAINTS

It is not only necessary but also, hopefully, encouraging to assess drivers, achievement, job satisfaction and talents. These are assets which propel you towards sculpting a career which is right for you. Now, however, we have to explore the dark side: that is, those factors which constrain and confine our choices.

For some people the careers which are right for them require capabilities which they simply don't have. Since the age of thirteen, Arthur had set his heart on becoming a fighter pilot in the Royal Air Force. But he wasn't accepted for training because he failed the eyesight test. He couldn't improve his colour vision, and had no choice but to accept defeat. After much grieving he searched for another career which utilized his drivers and talents, and decided to enter electronics engineering.

Sometimes a 'talent gap' can be insurmountable. Norma became a professional musician, playing the flute in a symphony orchestra. In spite of all her dedicated study she remained a good, average musician. She said: 'I realized that I didn't have outstanding talent. I just don't have the qualities to be a great musician. I guess it comes from genetics or astrology or something, but whatever it is, I didn't have it.' Norma reflected on her situation and decided that 'good, average' was not good enough to compensate for a demanding lifestyle. Instead of struggling on as a musician, she became a film editor, which uses some of her creative drive and allows her to have a full home life.

Careerists in the Richmond Survey were asked to consider very carefully the constraints which affected them. Key questions were: What factors constrain you? How do they influence your career decisions? Which constraints influence you most? Do you have experience of turning a constraint into a strength?

Respondents provided much useful data on their perceived constraints to freedom of career choice. I found that it was useful to categorize them under eight headings and to rank them in order of perceived importance:

- Poor health
- Wrong social class
- Inadequate or inappropriate education
- Gender stereotyping
- Wrong age
- Excessive commitments
- Poor self-concept
- Sparse geographic opportunities

These eight factors were all potential constraints, but each could also be a positive attribute. Consider, for example, social class. Paul spent much of his life travelling. Coming from an extremely well-connected and wealthy family, he's definitely upper class, so his connections enabled him to spend a decade casually exploring the world without causing any damage to his later lifestyle. Indeed, a dissolute youth was probably an advantage in his social circles.

Paul had an interesting viewpoint on constraints. He said: 'I never accept a barrier until I know it's solid. Barriers are doors in a long corridor. You have to see whether they will open if you turn the handle. If one of the doors is locked you have to try to pick the lock, or to find another way round, or to smash it down. Sometimes doors resist all your attempts to open them and there's no way round. Only if this happens will I accept that it's a genuine barrier.'

Significantly, it emerged that all eight constraints were

interrelated and interdependent. They were like boundary stakes supporting a fence round a house: if you move one stake, the whole fence changes shape. Constraints reduce the arena of choice. An example makes the point. Ken, aged thirty-eight, confided: 'I work all the hours God sends. In the next few years all this will change. I've got three teenaged children and life is very expensive right now. Soon the commitments will decrease and I can do what I really want and go to art school.' As Ken's commitments decrease, his opportunities to choose a new direction will increase and different constraints will influence his career.

As I mentioned, the eight constraints were ranked in order of perceived importance, as follows:

HEALTH

The survey respondents saw health as the most influential of all eight factors. Take the case of Margret, who suffered from a muscular wasting disease. Her career options were minimal, since she was unable to do anything physically demanding, and her horizons were limited by the sheer difficulty of getting around. Fortunately, most people are healthy enough. Health is crucial to those who have careers which demand physical prowess of one sort or another, which is a wider category than most people think. Sound recordists are dependent on hearing, teachers are dependent on their voices and postmen on their feet and legs. As well as unfortunate health problems, some careers are disturbed or destroyed by 'deliberate' ill health caused by such things as alcoholism and drug-taking.

Several respondents had experienced a significant deterioration of health during their careers. Interestingly, a bout of poor health was sometimes seen as beneficial in retrospect. Personal values about what was important were often reorientated by the experience of illness. For example, a heart attack in middle age can affect a whole lifestyle, usually by increasing awareness of the precious and privileged nature of human life.

The Richmond Study showed a direct connection between health and career management. People who were unwell in any way were likely to be confined by their ailment. This was generally true, but not always. Take Harold, a young man affected by Thalidomide before his birth. In spite of the fact that he virtually lacks his lower limbs, his ingenuity and willpower enabled him to become a highly accomplished craftsman. He was perhaps more resourceful than his contemporaries, demonstrating that some people grow stronger through overcoming adversity. Although the sample size was too small for sound generalization to be made, I came to the view that illnesses which drain physical energy or confuse the mind are the most damaging to careerists.

Survey respondents saw the current concern with leading a healthy life as directly relevant to effective career management. One reminded me that Chinese people only pay their doctors when they are healthy, believing that the purpose of medicine is to keep a person well and not simply to alleviate sickness. The active pursuit of 'wellness' was present in people who were largely satisfied with their career history. They took their lives seriously and cared about health, fitness and fulfilment. In particular, several respondents pointed out that demanding careers cause stress, and emotional development is essential in order to develop the skills and attitudes which enable stress to be maintained at a level which is stimulating but not debilitating.

Clearly, physical, emotional, intellectual and spiritual wellbeing is interrelated with the capacity to achieve and sustain a fulfilling career. As Alan said, 'What is the point of being consumed by any job and then thrown on to the scrap heap exhausted and useless?'

SOCIAL CLASS

The issue which was ranked as the second most important influence was social class. Whether we like it or not, human society is heavily stratified. In Great Britain, Europe and the USA the dominant dividing factor is socio-economic class. If the survey had been conducted in Bombay the Hindu caste system would have been the main dividing factor.

The concept of social class is indispensable for understanding Western career patterns. All societies are unequal, although the principle of division varies, ranging from religious belief and practice to economic circumstances. The rigidity of social boundaries also varies, from being absolute (like the South African apartheid system) to being more fluid and flexible (like in urban California). The prevailing system of social inequality affects how we live, what we do for a living and even how we think.

Children are born into a social context which greatly affects their chances in life. Wealthy and cultured parents treat their children very differently from the ways in which families living in multiracial slums treat theirs. The child knows nothing of choices already made on his or her behalf. The immediate environment seems natural, permanent and logical. Children aren't capable of being aware that their everyday social context is profoundly influencing their future life prospects.

Additional research conducted for this book included interviews with schoolchildren aged from fourteen to sixteen years. It was obvious that schools differed in the attitudes which they inculcated into their pupils. The most important factor from a career management viewpoint was that children in working-class schools talked about 'getting a job', while those in middle class schools were concerned with 'developing a career'. Some working-class children had very limited horizons, shown by statements like: 'I want to do shopwork' and 'I'd like to work with my hands'. A teacher in a working-class school described the prevailing attitudes in this way: 'Most of the kids here look on work as an extension of school. They want to get a job, but only as something that needs to be done to occupy them and provide money. There's little sense of progression for most of them. It's leave school, get a job if you can, and that's it. Perhaps the worst thing from the teacher's point of view is that a lot of the kids don't see any connection between achievement in school and achievement in life.'

When social scientists try to allocate a person to a social class they begin by asking what the individual's occupation is. Children are categorized by their fathers' occupations, and wives by their husbands'. For decades, sociologists have recognized that there is a close connection between occupation and social class. The edges are blurred and the fit is imperfect, but career development is clearly a class issue.

From a careful analysis of career biographies it appeared that social division affected those in the Richmond Survey in several ways.

First, membership of a particular social class is a mind-shaping experience. Richard, whose family is middle middle class, said: 'When I was at school all the kids expected to be army officers, doctors, lawyers, solicitors, accountants or some such established professional. We took it as being the natural thing for an adult to do.' This contrasted with Harry, whose family is respectable working class. He said, 'I went to a working-class school and no one really thought of a career. The kids were interested in getting a job or living off someone else. Frankly, a good proportion went into crime, unemployment, the army or pregnancy.'

Membership of a particular social class also leaves detectable stigmas, such as accent, which influence others, especially employers. Careers are more readily available to those who fit unspoken requirements. This was vividly demonstrated by the record of the interview with Winston, a twenty-three-year-old black man:

Interviewer: How did you get your first job?

Winston: Let me ask you a question. Do I look strong?

Interviewer: Yes; you must be over six foot tall and you look as if you're in great shape.

Winston: Well, that's the thing. I'm big. I'm black. I'm strong. I'm bold and I don't take no shit from no one.

Interviewer: Well?

Winston: Nobody likes to give a job to a strong black boy with a mouth. They want a docile white kid.

Interviewer: But you did get a job.

Winston: That's right. But not in your system. I got a job doing the fetching and carrying for a black radical newspaper.

Social classes are relatively closed categories: people prefer to mix with their own kind. Neighbourhoods attract those within certain class boundaries and, similarly, friendship patterns are related to class. Social circles offer opportunities for specific types of people; they partly determine what sociologists aptly call 'life chances'. This point was demonstrated by Katherine, whose family background is upper class. She said: 'Many of my best opportunities have occurred because I know someone who knows someone. I got a really good start at my present job because Daddy knew the chairman. It's not unfair. If I was a poor performer they would soon have me out. It's just that I get the opportunities when someone else wouldn't.'

Although social class has a profound influence on career patterns, the boundaries are not solid like walls round a prison. Mobility is both possible and accepted. Indeed, many careerists are primarily concerned with upward mobility, which sometimes means that they have to leave their class of origin and join a new class on their work/life journey.

Someone who understood the importance of social mobility well was Bob, who said: 'I came from a poor working-class family and I knew that this would be a millstone round my neck if I wanted to become a professional. So I deliberately changed my accent, mixed with middle-class people and became "cultured". Now it has become the way I am. I'm no longer a working-class boy and I can't really communicate with working-class people any longer. I'm true blue Conservative and live like one. It's a deliberate choice.'

The reality of social class was vividly brought home to me one day in southern California. Several internationally known consultants in the 'human potential movement' were talking about the new era of liberation of the human spirit. As the conversation went on, a Mexican maid came out and started to clean the patio, very discreetly skirting our discussion group. She held herself like an inferior and no one noticed as she polished and cleaned. When the task was completed she self-consciously approached the mistress of the house who was talking about 'transcendentalism'. The mistress paused, changed her tone, and said authoritatively: *'Los baños, ahora por favor.'* The group continued its earnest discussion on the evolution of mankind, while the maid did as she had been told and went off to clean the baths.

Once a person's social class is established, like a jelly in a mould, it's very difficult to change it. Class limits people's horizons in both the possible and the desirable. Perhaps the era when employers would select only members of a defined social class is largely over, but social class is still a major constraint.

EDUCATION

The issue which ranked third in importance was education in the widest sense. In some cases the absence of a specific educational achievement was a veto on membership of a group. Jack had failed his final architecture examinations three times and couldn't practise his preferred profession. He subsequently wandered into acting.

Career progress is greatly influenced by formal education, and professional or job training. But self-development and informal learning were sometimes more important than qualifications. Denese, now an editor, was a mathematics graduate who had edited the student newspaper in her university. The media world was far more impressed by her recreational activities than by her mathematics degree.

The survey showed that education influenced careers in many ways. Some people had obsolete or highly specialized skills and were disadvantaged by a declining level of demand for their talents. David, now unemployed, had been a draughtsman in a firm which bought a computer-aided design facility and halved its workforce. He's wisely using his enforced break from work to upgrade his skills. Not many people realized that education, like radioactivity, has a half-life. Unlike radioactive substances, however, the deterioration in the value of original qualifications is dependent on the social and technological environment. Arthur, one of several electronics specialists, said: 'My electronics qualifications were obsolete in months, not years. It's a major task just to keep up. No one really knows what to do with electronics specialists when they're over forty.'

There are clear links between educational success and social advance. Those people who had made a transition to a social class higher than that of their parents (thirty-nine individuals) felt that education was an essential aid to social mobility. Only in professions like popular music or property development was formal education eschewed. If a university student has working-class parents he or she almost inevitably moves into a different social class, which closes some doors but opens a new range of career opportunities.

A few respondents were from working-class homes and took blue collar jobs when they were sixteen. They began to make progress and in their twenties saw the possibility of a developmental career. They found that part-time education was a necessary adjunct and spent many evenings sitting in the local technical college. Education was a tool which could help them rise above the mass of their colleagues.

Academic achievement in itself is a necessary but inadequate qualification for entering most careers. Employers are interested in who the individual is, and what he or she can do, not simply in the qualifications possessed. They look for both formal education and the hard-to-define factor of personal development. Several respondents spoke of the importance of exploring their own nature, knowing what they want and freeing their energy. There is a link between self-knowledge and career success.

GENDER

The issue which ranked fourth was gender. Sexual factors play an important role in constraining career choices, although there's a slow movement towards greater equality between the sexes.

Important distinctions remain, however. For example, despite some encouragement, girls still largely avoid science subjects at school and move into serving roles. They give up their careers to have children and achieve lower income and status. By 1984 in Britain women were still only earning 74 per cent of the average male wage. Of course, there are many exceptions, but historically careers have been a male preoccupation. According to a study by the National Council for Civil Liberties, in 1982 women comprised 40 per cent of the workforce in the UK but 60 per cent of them worked in clerical, welfare and education areas.

Women in the Richmond Study made the following general points about women's careers:

- Girls are less inclined to 'think career' and much more inclined to 'get a job'
- Lack of personal development and self-assertiveness are the primary blocks to female achievement
- Greater commitment to promoting human welfare means that women are prepared to discount self-aggrandizement for the sake of the wellbeing of others
- Problems due to having both domestic and work roles (especially on a shoestring budget) are considerable, and sometimes overwhelming
- Isolation and deep frustration are relatively commonplace among women
- The acquisition of power for its own sake interests only a small minority of women
- Lack of social appreciation of the role of housewife and mother means that some women who choose to perform these roles feel like members of a lower caste

In spite of these social and historical disadvantages, there are an increasing number of career women as distinct from the bulk of working women who 'have a job'. Yet there are still not many of them; for example, in 1985 only 2.4 per cent of the members of the British Institute of Management were female. It's indisputable that women are capable. Some earn substantial wages: in 1984 20 per cent of women in Great Britain earned as much as, or more than, their husbands.

A prestigious career is almost always regarded as a blessing by a man, but some of the women in the Richmond Survey felt ambiguous about their apparently outstanding careers, and resentful that their energies were diverted from things such as their homes and families, which they now felt were basically more important. Not all women are seething with resentment. Several surveys have demonstrated that most women say they are 'satisfied' by their careers, and that they put their domestic commitments first.

Gender also affects male careers. Employers tend to be demanding, and they're not prepared to consider the consequences of job requirements on a man's lifestyle. This can greatly interfere with family life. The time in a man's career when he is acquiring credits for the future is often the same period during which his wife and young family most need attention and support.

The gender issue raises many questions. The thesis of this book is that there is no such thing as a good career in absolute terms; it all depends on what you want and need. From this it follows that the disparity between male and female career patterns can be judged in two ways: either as a totally acceptable manifestation of biological differences, or as an outdated relic of an unfair past. Psychologists debate whether differences in attitudes, values, behaviour and needs between the sexes arise from basic physiological differences or from social conditioning. This issue is important in a practical way. If you believe that people of both sexes are basically the same, then a person's gender should have no effect on their career choices or opportunities. On the other hand, if you believe that there are real and important differences, then the careers of men and women should reflect their fundamentally different natures.

It was Betty who helped me to see the dilemma clearly. She said, 'Like everyone else I have been influenced by well-meaning propaganda. All sorts of people tell me what to think and how to feel as a woman. Yes, I was affected by the feminist movement and spent many hours with a group of strident but amiable women discussing our collective misfortune. Now I am less doctrinaire. I realized that being a woman was just one aspect of me as an individual and it was foolish and destructive to become a soldier in a feminist army.'

As the Richmond Survey interviews proceeded, I became persuaded that gender issues were significant managerial challenges. Men found it difficult to devote sufficient time to their work, home and recreation. Women had managerial problems in reconciling domestic and work demands. Those individuals who had found a balance between the contradictory pulls seemed to:

- Give weight to the internal emotional messages (inner directed)
- Enjoy the experience of being a man or a woman (bold acceptance)
- Be very careful about making long-term commitments (prudent foresight)
- Avoid being influenced by social fashions (sceptical to persuasion)
- Seek deep satisfaction of their wants and needs (driver conscious)
- Admit their dependence on others (accept vulnerability)

Few people are able to discount gender issues totally. Employers are sexist in attitude and employees are sexist in behaviour. Everyone needs to discover what they need to do to fulfil their sexual identity and then allow themselves to flourish. This affects the choice of career and creates career management problems.

AGE

Ths issue which ranked fifth in importance was age. Age is a limitation for everyone except those who are really outstanding. Work lives were largely divided into three distinct stages: first learning, then work, then recreation. There is no real logic in this:

from some points of view it would be far more sensible to fuse these three elements. But that's how it is. A few people start major new phases of their careers well after the conventionally accepted age. Winston Churchill, for example, began to paint as a profitable recreation after the age of forty, and Ronald Reagan became President of the United States in his seventieth year. But we can't base our careers on a few rare exceptions. The people in the Richmond Survey found that years are like financial capital, and each person had to address this question: 'Where should my years be invested for the best return?' For the older members of the Richmond sample, age was becoming increasingly significant. In advanced years it became the primary factor.

My colleague Ezra Kogan has watched the unfolding of many careers and says, with some cynicism: 'Age is everything.' In most formalized careers, 'windows of opportunity' exist by which a person can enter a career or make a jump. Such windows of opportunity effectively limit almost everyone. Petra said: 'It's like standing on a moving walkway. For a time you can get off but then the opportunity has gone past. If you're lucky a new opportunity comes, but eventually the opportunities dry up.' We can see an example in medicine. It's virtually impossible for a middle-aged person – unless he or she has extraordinary credentials – to train as a doctor.

Respondents in the Richmond Survey identified eight 'career choice points' which are sequential and related to age. These are moments at which fundamental strategic decisions are made. We can compare them in importance to a traveller's decision about how to undertake a long journey. The first and most important choice is whether to travel by plane, train, boat, car or bicycle. Once the traveller has decided on which mode of transport to use, there are quite a few significant tactical decisions to be made, but they're all within the context of the main strategic decision. The cyclist has to decide whether to carry a sleeping bag, and the air passenger must decide what flight to catch, but these are minor decisions compared with the fundamental choice about which method of travel to use.

Let's take a look at the eight 'choice points'.

What Constrains Me?

Choice Point One – What School? (up to 16 years)

Career paths begin very early. Many people would say that they begin even before a child is born. The subjects in which a child specializes at school inevitably guide him or her towards certain careers. This happens in obvious ways; for example, non-science students rarely go into technical occupations. It also happens insidiously in that disciplines influence attitudes, perspectives and thought processes. The foundation of a career is laid before we are mature enough to understand what's going on.

Next, young people start to plan their futures. When I was only nine I decided that I wanted to be an author . . . one day perhaps! Dreams like this have to be validated and transformed into workable options. The young person has to make vocational choices to prepare himself or herself for the future. At this time of life, habits of work and attitudes towards it are established.

Key issue: the degree to which talents are recognized and developed.

Choice Point Two – Whether to Qualify? (16–20 years)

After completing their basic schooling (at about sixteen years of age), some young people become shelf-fillers in supermarkets, while others settle down to another five years of full-time education. Some become pregnant and/or marry, while other practically-minded individuals begin an apprenticeship.

In this phase, which is associated with late adolescence, young people discover their own interests, drivers, talents and limitations. They meet people who have careers that they themselves would like, and use them as models. Students are well advised to maintain an adequate level of accomplishment so that they keep their options open. Part-time and holiday jobs provide useful experience of work.

Key issue: exploiting educational advantages.

Choice Point Three – What Organization? (16–23 years)

Sooner or later young people leave education and join an organization. At least, this used to be the pattern. Today's unemployment blights many careers even before they begin. The search for a first job is a crucial event. Young people must learn the skills of surveying the market, applying for jobs or training, and being a successful interviewee. Not all jobs are developmental or progressive. The young careerist must learn to discriminate between different job offers according to their quality.

Becoming a member of an organization is a social transition of considerable importance. The young person has to absorb new expectations, customs, traditions and pecking orders. He or she often has a struggle to be accepted, and has to learn the informal rules which govern selection to more interesting, powerful, senior or rewarding roles.

Key issue: entry into a progressive role.

Choice Point Four – How High to Aim? (16–30 years)

A person must decide how far he or she wishes to progress. Career foundations are firmly laid before the age of thirty. The question is: 'How far do I wish to go in my working life?'

People who want to build a developmental career have to develop their skills and competencies during the first phase of their working lives. On the psychological level, this phase is characterized by the growth of real self-confidence. A decade without achievement would be disastrous. The best time to acquire breadth of experience is before commitments such as a family or mortgage make it difficult to move.

The training period corresponds with coming to terms with the shock of being at work and the problems of adjusting to new disciplines and demands. Many young people feel themselves to be extremely knowledgeable; they need to learn the boundaries of their competence. Relating well to superiors is especially important. As the reality of organizational life gradually becomes clearer, the trainee needs to become an effective contributor to the organization and to begin to establish a track record.

Key issue: level of aspiration.

Choice Point Five – Work Life Balance? (30–40 years)

Between thirty and forty the career pattern has largely been established and acquires a momentum of its own. The supermarket shelf-filler becomes more and more limited by the job, whilst professionals or executives gain new competencies by undertaking stretching challenges.

By the time the career is firmly established, people have usually developed totally independent personal lives. Family and home become increasingly important to them and they have to make difficult choices about where to invest their time.

Performance is centrally important during this period of life. People take on more demanding responsibilities, acquire and use special skills and abilities, and put a lot of effort into becoming effective and learning how to get things done. A high degree of commitment is expected from them. People in this phase of their lives gain from working close to experienced and high-performing older workers.

People in senior roles need to choose between a generalist or specialist career route. They must take action to maintain a high level of up-to-date expertise. It is important that they find ways of being noticed by powerful people. The individual becomes more clearly differentiated from others, and learns to cope with complexity and scale.

Key issue: performance and fulfilment.

Choice Point Six – Whether to Redirect? (38–45 years)

By the age of forty, half the careerist's working life is over, and he or she can look back on considerable experience. A new question dominates early middle age: 'What am I going to do with the rest of my life?' People have to rethink their careers and validate the decisions they originally made. They sometimes decide to make radical changes. There are often new opportunities for personal growth. But career prospects may be degenerative as well; for example, a grudging realization that a career plateau has been reached, perhaps followed by a gentle or even precipitous decline.

The age of forty has become infamous as the time during which people are likely to experience what has become known as the 'mid-life crisis'. The term is accurate. This stage in a person's life provokes a major reassessment of many aspects of life and work. A lot of people find that a new seriousness enters their lives at this stage. Psychologically, the realization of their mortality plays a part. There is a growing recognition that 'you are who you are', and a deep-seated confidence can flow from the realizations which emerge from this traumatic period.

People going through this stage of their lives have to re-draw career horizons in the light of current reality. Increasingly, they have to cope with competition from able younger people. It becomes harder to change jobs because prospective employers often don't give older people a chance, writing them off simply on the basis of age.

Key issue: clarity about aims.

Choice Point Seven – How to Contribute? (40–60 years)

Mid-career redirection is a time of turbulence which is followed by a relatively calm period. Principles and values frequently become more important to people in this phase. Their lives are often worthy and based on regular habits. From an outsider's view this may appear to be a period of declining energy.

Successful careerists will enjoy this phase of working life, which lasts until near retirement. They adopt statesman roles by becoming mentors, and enjoy developing other people's talents. They continue to acquire capabilities. People at this stage often need to make judgements of a political nature, which perhaps include difficult choices about values and strategies. They also have to consider long-term horizons.

People who rate their careers as 'unsuccessful' adjust differently. They grudgingly come to terms with their experience, perhaps seeing work as a kind of prison sentence. Issues like finding satisfying hobbies are important. Those without a satisfying career find the experience of this phase dangerous: it's all too easy for decline to set in.

Key issue: statesmanship or decline.

Choice Point Eight – How to Opt Out? (55–70 years)

The period of late middle age brings a new critical question: 'How do I prepare materially and psychologically for stopping work?' Most people accept the concept of retirement, which is, of course, a major transition in life. Some options are closed while others are opened. Wise decision-making can result in major benefits to the life of the individual.

People going through this phase find that their lives are less dominated by the requirements of children and the pressure of work. There is time to develop reflective and responsive pursuits.

On a practical level, people must make decisions about finance, housing, and retirement. One thing they might do is to become more involved in their local community life.

Those who have had active and involved careers may find it difficult to accept reduced levels of authority, responsibility and influence. Their competence may also decline, for reasons of physical or mental deterioration, or of obsolescent knowledge. Retirement threatens their self-concept. A retired person has less status than a senior job-holder. It's not easy for people to find vehicles for their abilities and energies when they're retired.

Key issue: reassessment of potential.

COMMITMENTS

The issue which ranked sixth in importance was commitments. These were obligations to others, most often family but also friends, communities or financial institutions. Adults become bound by obligations. Bob said to me: 'I can do anything I like so long as I earn £30,000 a year.' His commitment to raising his children was more important than any concern for personal satisfaction.

We have to see careers in context. Sitting opposite Alan in a restaurant discussing the choices he faced in his career, I asked the following questions:

- What is your family situation like?
- How many financial obligations do you have?
- How important is your family to you?
- Who looks after your home?
- How independent is your wife?
- How much time do you like to spend with your children?
- How important are your sports and hobbies to you?
- What commitments do you have to other members of your family?
- Do you have any other commitments which influence your career choices?

Questions like these are crucial. Careers should never be determined without reference to the individual's lifestyle. Ideally, a career should support a way of life rather than dominate it. Those who rate their careers as successful speak of mental, emotional, spiritual, physical, material and moral development being interrelated and embracing family, friendship and achievement. Even heavy commitments outside are often positive and deliberately chosen. It's short-sighted to see a career as an end in itself. Some of the most disturbing career review discussions that I've experienced were with people who had devoted a great deal to their careers and then woken up to the realization that they had invested so much of their lifetime energy in a cause which didn't fully satisfy them.

As survey respondents acquired commitments, their self-perception changed. Decisions that would have been taken alone before were discussed by the whole family. People were more likely to see risks as threats rather than desirable adventures. Once people acquired commitments, caution was a common thread running through their lives. Such careerists protected their leisure time, recognizing that commitments are time-hungry. This is especially true of spouses and children who, quite properly, need significant and regular attention.

Most of those who took part in the survey believed that families only thrive in a stable environment. This severely limits career choices for some people. David was a ship's officer in his early career and said: 'After I married, it became clear to me that I couldn't carry on a career at sea. My wife said, "I want you in our bed at nights – no buts." That was my choice: her, or boats.' Roger, a civil engineer, was offered an interesting career move which would mean travelling overseas regularly. His first thoughts were of his family life. He said: 'I want to take the job, but I've got to think long and hard. The wife and kids come first. I won't do anything which might damage my family.'

For many people, financial obligations constrain choices and make it seem less desirable to jump off one career ladder and start at the bottom of another. Some people find that they are motivated by financial needs. Katherine, a highly successful marketing and sales executive, said rather cynically: 'We found that the best motivator for a salesman on the road was a big mortgage and an acquisitive wife.' Not everyone is cowed by commitments; for some they act as a spur. Having obligations turns work into something more than a game.

People find chosen commitments easier to cope with than those which are forced on them by circumstances. Walter's wife suffered from extreme post-natal depression, which was one of the reasons for their divorce. She left the children in his care. He accepted the burden, but painfully came to terms with the understanding that, for the next decade, he would only be able to take well-paid jobs without extensive travel obligations. Of course, people who had financial or family resources were better able to weather such storms than relatively isolated nuclear families who depend on good health and reasonable fortune.

SELF-CONCEPT

The issue which ranked seventh was the way in which people saw themselves: that is, their self-concept. This topic seemed so basic to me that it gave me the impetus for Step One of this book. People's definitions of their own abilities and characters are a primary determinant of their behaviour. This has often been demonstrated. For example, recent research into criminality has shown that people who lack confidence are much more likely to become victims of street crime than those who appear, by their movements and behaviour, to be resourceful and confident.

Several survey respondents admitted that they wouldn't pursue particular aspirations because of 'lack of confidence', saying: 'I don't know, it's too big a step for me.' This was an illustration of the fact that mental images (called 'mind sets') affect behaviour. Mind sets are very powerful. They mean, for example, that if people consider themselves to be ungainly and awkward they will behave as if this were an objective fact. If people like this were able to give themselves permission to be socially confident then their whole demeanour would change.

A few respondents (only four, in fact) felt that their self-image was the strongest limitation on their career choices. But the majority of respondents disagreed. This difference in outlook may be explained by the subconscious nature of mind sets. Some psychologists aptly describe self-concept as being like a mental map. The scale of the map and the features shown on it are drawn up by the person, and he or she perceives this as accurate. In fact, the map may be totally illusory or may show features and frontiers where none actually exist.

Self-image was sometimes a limitation because it led to over-inflated egos. Respondents reported that some of their colleagues suffered from grandiose estimations of their own capabilities; this led to feelings of outraged indignation at the fact that their talents were unrecognized. None of the fifty-three respondents felt that this fault applied to them, although the law of averages would suggest that some of the group would suffer from the delusions which they accused others of exhibiting.

Careerists are well advised to seek a realistic self-image which isn't bound by unreal inner doubts. Nor should they allow their egos to become over-inflated or to contain even minor illusions of unwarranted grandeur. The best balance of opposites would seem to be an attitude which combines confidence and humility.

GEOGRAPHY

The issue which ranked lowest was geography. Perhaps this was because the survey was conducted in an affluent area. One of the characteristics of an unfair world is that some people are much more fortunately situated than others. The Mercedes-Benz franchisee in Hollywood has a much more lucrative asset than the same franchisee in the black South African township of Soweto.

Most respondents considered their own region or country to be the boundary of their aspirations. Other countries, especially those in which the people spoke a different language, were considered to be 'beyond the pale'. Exceptions to this included highly regarded professionals like Luke, or those who had a loose connection with established society such as Desmond, the poet and writer.

In spite of attractions which a move from one place to another may have, pulling up one's roots is rarely painless, often traumatic and sometimes disastrous. New environments are unfamiliar and tend to reject outsiders. Skills for adaptation to novel situations are thinly spread. Not many people are used to starting from scratch in an unfamiliar world. Fortunately, we can learn to make changes by experimenting and reflecting on the results. Venturesome holidays are an example of a deliberate strategy of trying new things and learning survival skills.

I came to believe that geography is a much underrated influence on careers. People who had positioned themselves where their talents were wanted had many more opportunities than those who tried to sell their abilities in unfavourable conditions.

The influence of geography on opportunity has always been understood by people living in deprived areas. Recently, 132 bachelors in a remote Spanish village advertised for women; there were no local girls available because they had all gone to work in larger towns. For generations the Irish have left their own country to seek opportunities around the world. Murphys and O'Reillys can be found in Australia, Tierra del Fuego, and Hong Kong. It makes sense, therefore, for careerists to locate themselves in a place which provides the opportunities they seek.

You've now read the constraints as described and ranked by the respondents in the Richmond Survey. No doubt you find some echoes in your own situation. On the next page you will find a project which helps you reflect on the actual factors that constrain your career. Complete the project before you proceed to Step Seven.

YOUR INNER AND OUTER CONSTRAINTS

This project will help you explore the inner and outer constraints which reduce your career choices. It has two sections. Answer Part One quickly by brainstorming objections and listing them as shown, then methodically complete Part Two.

Part One

Why can't you be a:	*Reasons why not*
film star?	
karate teacher?	
university professor?	
television producer?	
student?	
ship owner?	
farmer?	
professional soccer player?	

Why can't you be a:	*Reasons why not*
writer?	
blacksmith?	
coal miner?	
striptease artist?	
ski instructor?	
dog breeder?	
airline pilot?	
lathe operator?	
brain surgeon?	
circus clown?	
poet?	
insurance salesperson?	

Part Two

Reflect on your life, background and situation. Consider each of the eight constraints described in the last chapter and ask yourself whether they affect you. Record your answers in the space provided.

1. My health constrains my career in the following ways:

   (a)

   (b)

   (c)

   (d)

   (e)

2. My social class constrains my career in the following ways:

   (a)

   (b)

   (c)

   (d)

   (e)

3. My education constrains my career in the following ways:

   (a)

   (b)

   (c)

   (d)

   (e)

4. My gender constrains my career in the following ways:

   (a)

   (b)

   (c)

   (d)

   (e)

5. My age constrains my career in the following ways:

   (a)

   (b)

   (c)

   (d)

   (e)

6. My commitments constrain my career in the following ways:

   (a)

   (b)

   (c)

   (d)

   (e)

7. My self-concept constrains my career in the following ways:

   (a)

   (b)

   (c)

   (d)

   (e)

8. My geographical location constrains my career in the following ways:

   (a)

   (b)

   (c)

   (d)

   (e)

9. Look back over your answers to the last eight items and then ask yourself: If I wanted to change my career direction with every fibre of my being then what would stop me?

   (a)

   (b)

   (c)

   (d)

   (e)

STEP SEVEN

What Organization Suits Me?

> 'Mid pleasures and palaces though we may roam,
> Be it ever so humble, there's no place like home.'
>
> *J. H. Payne*

WHAT ORGANIZATIONAL SETTING?

In the first six steps of managing your own career we looked at *you* from various angles. Hopefully, you're now better informed and more optimistic; feel stronger but realize that there are real limitations to your possibilities. You have reflected upon the most important personal factors which determine the direction and scope of your career choices.

This section takes a different perspective. Here we're going to look outwards at the world of work. This is an essential preparation for career management. The latter half of this book moves towards action planning, which has to take into account the realities of the world of work. Then you will be better placed to devise a career which is a good marriage between yourself and your environment.

Organization has a profound influence on career patterns. Let's have a look at Salina's case to give us an idea of the kind of conditions we face in the outside world. Salina worked in her father's dress shop for several years after leaving school. Later, she virtually ran the shop, managing the administration and helping her father to buy new merchandise. When the shop was sold she joined Herbert and Karl, a national retail chain store group. Salina said:

'It was a tremendous shock to join a big company. When I worked with my dad I did all the tasks. In H & K I couldn't do anything. Everything had to be done by the book. They even wanted me to wear certain kinds of clothes to work. I hated the regimentation and lack of freedom.' Many respondents gave similar accounts of the enormous influence that organizations have on their working lives.

For many people, a career is synonymous with organizational life. Many career choices concern how best to proceed through the sometimes difficult terrain of an organization. Position, power, status and security: these are all payoffs which are largely derived from organizations. Indeed, in the Richmond Survey, the majority (67 per cent) answered the question 'How do you see your future career developing?' by talking about organizational status levels. For example, Frank said: 'I see myself as a grade eight by the time I am thirty, and grade seven by age thirty-four.' There was no mention of job contribution or job content; for Frank, hierarchy was the most important index of success. Aspirations like his can only be met within an organizational setting.

Organizations differ greatly in terms of their structure. Some are monolithic and highly predictable while others are constantly changing shape, rather like disturbed amoebas. While in one enterprise nobody gets power until he is gnarled and distinguished by grey hair (women don't seem to count), in another executives look as if they should still be going to college and there is a liberal sprinkling of elegant young women in the top jobs. Careers differ according to their particular organizational context.

Organizations mould people's attitudes and behaviour to suit their prevailing style. Sociologists call this the 'socialization process'. The character or 'culture' of an organization shapes thought processes and behavioural patterns. Some organizational cultures are more congenial to particular careers than others.

Respondents in the Richmond Survey spoke about organizations at length. In essence they asked two questions. Firstly, what structure of organization offers me the best opportunities? Secondly, what organizational culture will I fit into?

To answer these questions we need to have a deeper

understanding of the characteristics of organizations. An overview of current organizational sociology helps the careerist to choose which organizational context is likely to suit his or her driving forces and talents.

Organizations are the most powerful tool known to man. They offer work to perhaps a billion people. There is no other means of combining human talents and resources to get complex things done. An effective organization is a superb achievement, as important to mankind as a work of art or a scientific invention. If you just take a few moments to reflect on the amount of good done by the International Red Cross, you'll see exactly what I mean.

We can consider organizations independently of the people who work for them. Their effectiveness is measured by the extent to which organizational aims and goals are reached, not by the fulfilment of employees' desires and aspirations. Whether these aims are worthwhile is largely determined by customers, not by employees. In the end, organizations thrive or die depending on their competitiveness or perceived value in society.

From the organizational viewpoint people are both a curse and a blessing. They are costly to maintain. Anyone who has looked into the accounts of a major charity knows that vast sums are spent on the apparently simple task of getting funds from the giver to the receiver. Most of the costs go on human resources. Yet in spite of the expense and unreliability of people, organizations need them. Shortages of adequate skills can be catastrophic. There have been many cases where a once successful organization has failed because the key roles weren't being performed by people who were fully competent. The guardians and stewards of organizations have ambivalent attitudes towards people. They dislike human nature's unpredictability and irascibility, preferring machines to perform predictable functions. At the same time, the power-holders in organizations know that they are dependent on people, who can be uniquely creative, flexible, diligent and skilful.

Top managers see their roles as similar to those of head gardeners. They know that unless gardens are constantly tended, they'll eventually turn into wild and unkempt tangles of verdure.

So they cut, dig and prune; a process which sometimes favours people, and sometimes not. The primary objective is to construct an organization which is fit for its purpose. Senior managers have discovered that there's no universal formula or doctrinaire set of assumptions which can be applied to organizational design. An organization which is appropriate for a university is quite different from one which is best suited to a retail store. A rock band is different again. Organizational design is as individual as the purpose for which it's designed.

The size of an organization is a primary determinant of the type of workplace it is. Small and large organizations are distinctly different from one another. Since large organizations have the most scope for different roles, let's have a detailed look at them. They are necessary to perform huge tasks (like mass production of cars) and they benefit from economies of scale. Such structures become highly specialized and develop five distinct categories of employee.

1. OPERATORS

These are the people who actually control the machines, complete documents, use tools, drive trucks and so on. They may be highly skilled, like an optical lens technician, or marginally qualified, like a table clearer in a hamburger restaurant. Operator careers attract those who score high in Expertise, Affiliation and Security driving forces with Working With Things or Applied Science talents. In general they are low status and fairly low paid. Careers of this sort are vulnerable to automation.

2. MANAGERS

Whenever more than a handful of people work together, it's necessary to develop a management function. Someone has to set objectives, monitor progress, co-ordinate activities, make plans and take the right action when things go wrong. Management is a relatively new craft (a combination of science, art and experience) which has become a major opportunity for careerists. Managers always arrange themselves in a hierarchy to reduce overload for those at the top, so there's a progressive structure. Management jobs are demanding, fragmented and responsible. They call for specialized intellectual competencies, emotional resilience and a relentless search for better ways to do things. Careers in management may attract people who score high in the Material Rewards, Power/Influence and Status driving forces, with Adminstration/Management talents. In the next twenty years many middle management jobs will disappear as fifth-generation computers take over some intelligent functions.

3. ANALYSTS

Large organizations invariably become extremely complex, so they employ specialists to establish efficient procedures and devise systems which bring their complexity under control. Consider, for example, the difficulties inherent in manufacturing a computer or putting on an opera. Only by using technical disciplines and scientific management techniques can such large tasks be successfully accomplished. Analysts have advisory roles but their expertise gives them enormous influence. Occupations such as those of systems analysts, accountants, business planners and personnel managers fall into this category. Analyst careers may attract those who score high in the Creativity, Expertise and Security driving forces, with Applied Science and Administration/ Management talents. Every indication points to this being a growth area for careerists.

4. SUPPORT STAFF

No organization devotes all its energies to production. Someone has to type the letters and keep the floors swept, make sure that the rooms are warm and supply food in the dining room. Those who perform support functions tend to have low status and fewer career routes open to them. People who occupy roles of this type are more likely to describe themselves as 'having a job' than as 'having a career', although there are efforts to improve the status of support people. People in this category are also likely to become victims of mechanization or, more recently, privatization. Support staff careers may attract those who score high in the Expertise, Affiliation and Security driving forces, with talents in Caring/Helping and Working With Things.

5. DIRECTORS

An organization has to maintain a corporate identity and channel its energies towards achievements. This role, which Stafford Beer calls the 'brain of the firm', is performed by those at the apex of the organization, the directors. Their role is to formulate corporate strategy, then to make basic decisions about direction and capability. Director careers may attract those who score high in the Material Rewards, Power/Influence, Search for Meaning and Status driving forces, with Administration/Management and Self-Expression as talents. Directors have high prestige and will continue to be needed even in the highly automated organizations of the future.

These are the five categories of employees within organizations. They occur in all organizations, except the very smallest. But this doesn't help us to categorize organizations in ways which assist people in finding the best context for their career. We need a way to differentiate between various types of organization, and I acknowledge the work of Henry Mintzberg, *The Structuring of Organizations* (Prentice-Hall, Englewood Cliffs 1980), in developing these concepts.

ORGANIZATION TYPES

Organizations can be categorized into five types. Each has a distinct character and offers particular career patterns. The five types of organization are:

1. SIMPLE STRUCTURES

Small businesses (or larger organizations in crisis) thrive under clear 'hands-on' leadership by a boss. Complexity, excess staff, over-elaborate systems and formality are enemies. The organization must be kept simple and flexible, with the boss in control. He or she takes decisions, seizes opportunities and aggressively confronts the world. But beware: the simple structure is the most risky of all, since it hinges on the health and drive of one person. Expansion is limited, since the lack of formal organization prevents the management of large tasks.

In small organizations careers are divided into those for leaders and those for followers. The boss has an opportunity to gain high Material Rewards, substantial Power/Influence, personal Meaning and ample Autonomy. Followers have much more limited career options. Unless there's considerable expansion, hierarchical progress is given only a little space. But simple structures are often multifaceted and diverse. People enjoy a surprising variety of work, and feel close to the hub, so they see work as more meaningful than in a large organization.

Simple structures are frequently established by independent professionals like solicitors or doctors. There the head of the organization is a qualified member of a traditional profession. There's no formal career structure; everything is done on a personal basis.

Slightly different simple structures are created by quasi-professionals like photographers who lack formalized training and whose definition of job content is much more vague. Specialized expertise, however, is highly valued. The customer plays an important role in defining success.

Louis is the owner of several businesses, and one of them has a typical simple structure. World Food Ltd is a mail order company which sells foreign-language cookery books mostly to restaurants which specialize in foreign food. Louis said: 'I run the business, and I've got seven ladies to help me. One of the girls works the computer, three work as packers, one lady orders products from the overseas publishers and two of them process orders and send out catalogues. Everyone does whatever's necessary to get the job done. There's no job demarcation here. I make the decisions about the stock, marketing, contracts, prices and so on, and I check to see that everyone is doing their job properly. It's a nice little company. The girls come to me with any questions.' This is typical of work in simple structures.

Perhaps the simplest structure of all applies to those with vocations, like poets or vicars. Here the discipline is everything. There is a strong personal commitment. Entry requirements depend on the individual mastery of the specialization. A very high order of expertise can be expected.

2. LARGE PRODUCTION ORGANIZATIONS

Some organizations, like airlines or post offices, have many routine tasks to perform predictably time and time again. Jobs become highly specialized and training is essential. There are rules and regulations everywhere. Communication and decision-making are formalized, elaborate and intricate. A network of specialized departments emerges, each of which is led by managers who are expert in their particular disciplines. Specialists like work study analysts, accountants, quality controllers and planners proliferate; without them, the organization would collapse into chaos. Managers are 'obsessed' with control, trying to measure all variables and to eliminate uncertainty.

Although the production type of organization is technically efficient, there are latent conflicts which threaten productivity. People at the lower end of the organization find all the controls and regulations dehumanizing. Tension mounts, and often all that top managers can do is alleviate or bottle up potential troubles; they find it virtually impossible to introduce a humanistic environment into a system which is essentially mechanistic.

Careers in a production organization arc attractive to people who enjoy formalization and standardization. Only the directors have considerable discretion and power, and they insist on rationality and discipline further down the line.

Production organizations are large, hierarchical and predictable. Careers tend to evolve along social class lines, especially where there are still many blue collar jobs to be done. There is a wide variety of analytical roles available in larger production organizations. Progress is punctuated by formal training courses. Discipline, standard-setting and effective human resource management are widely valued. Those with Administration/ Management talents and Security and Status as career drivers tend to be attracted. People with strong needs for Autonomy or Self-Expression often feel oppressed by the rule-bound culture. The organization has built-in inertia, so it has to be constantly kicked like an unwilling horse. Highly developed political skills are an acknowledged asset.

William is a production manager, and his career experience reflects the kind of organization in which he operates. He said: 'I live my life by schedules. I've got one of those diaries which tells me what to do every fifteen minutes and I really need it. I'm so structured that I know when it's time to go to the toilet. My office is full of charts. I measure everything that moves. I hate surprises. Life should go like clockwork and I constantly try to make it work smoothly. It's a real challenge to get something done but we are constantly experimenting. I like to think that I'm fine-tuning a machine. My job would only suit someone who respects order, but a pussycat won't do – you have to push and shove the machine to get it to go.' This is typical of work in a large production organization.

3. PROFESSIONAL ORGANIZATIONS

Police forces, universities, hospitals and accounting firms share a common feature: they all require highly trained individuals to meet complex and unpredictable requirements from the customer. This form of organization is dependent on the competence of highly educated and skilled workers who must be trusted to do the job in a 'professional' way. All doctors can, we trust, be expected to complete a thorough diagnosis when a patient arrives with a complaint, but the procedures naturally vary from patient to patient. Doctors cannot be supervised or programmed all the time – that would be enormously expensive and counter-productive – so the organization provides an environment which sets basic standards and then enables the professionals to get on with their work.

Careers in professional organizations begin with a comparatively enormous amount of training and education. Professional skills and attitudes take years to accumulate and must then be regularly updated. Professionals have to learn to avoid both simplistic rule-making and its opposite, abdication from responsibility. Administrators develop a steering and co-ordinating role. Power is largely decentralized and the overall leadership style is persuasive rather than autocratic. For this reason, it's difficult to determine who is really in charge. The professional organization often provides deeply satisfying careers but the lack of a strong central organization unfortunately means that much decision-making emerges from political intrigue. Influence rather than rational argument can rule the day. Innovation, which requires the co-operation of colleagues, is notoriously difficult to orchestrate. In fact, creative thinking often fails to flourish in such organizations, since they prefer to work along time-proven lines. Change can only take place with the willing co-operation of many independent people, and it often proceeds with an almost painful slowness. It's difficult or impossible to manage by objectives, since the outputs are often intangible. However, in spite of all the disadvantages, organizations which require people to perform a wide variety of unpredictable and complex tasks have no option but to place control in the hands of the professional. Nothing else has been proven to work.

Career structures are organized into professional structures, which have rigid entry requirements, fastidious grading and intensive training. Support structures enable professionals to do their work. People with Search for Meaning and Autonomy as drivers are attracted to professions, and their talents may well lie in Caring/Helping. A high level of ability is required and the profession is recognized outside the boundaries of the organization. Support services offer alternative career structures, but this is seen as a lower status occupation.

Ann, a teacher, works in a professional organization. She said: 'My school authorities are very careful about who they employ. They only take graduates and insist on good teacher training qualifications. Once in the classroom, you're expected to be able to work alone. I set my own standards, make the decisions and cope with the problems. My head of department is really a senior counsellor. We try to have a professional relationship. The career structure is a pain. Seniority is the main criterion, and opportunities for different work are limited. Teaching suits responsible people who are capable of making their own decisions.' This is typical of work in a professional organization.

4. DECENTRALIZED ORGANIZATIONS

Most large profit-making organizations have learned that over-centralization is clumsy, so they evolve into specialized mini-organizations streamlined for specific markets. Semi-independent units devoted to a limited range of products are co-ordinated by headquarters which is responsible for directing the overall stategy.

In decentralized organizations, decision-making is pushed downwards and independent divisions are formed, each having a full complement of analysts and support staff. This is expensive in overheads, but it allows units to be independently accountable.

Each unit or division develops its own goals which it negotiates with headquarters. Quantitative measures are required; without them, control cannot be exercised. Headquarters allows a lot of freedom but carefully monitors results. Much day-to-day authority is given to middle managers whose skills are critical, and they receive extensive training and 'indoctrination' to ensure that their decision-making is of a consistently high quality.

A sympathetic use of both carrot and stick best describes the relationship between headquarters and division. Headquarters retains control over strategic planning, allocation of financial resources, control systems, appointment of key personnel, basic research and formulation of key policies. The units focus their attention on the markets they know, and endeavour to exploit them. The division tries to behave like a blinkered horse pounding towards the winning post.

Decentralized organizations have particular appeal for people who are seeking entrepreneurial careers without excessive personal risk, since they have the following advantages:

- Capital is allocated by headquarters so is not the personal responsibility of the directors
- Running a unit allows management skills to be developed
- Risk is spread – managers can move to other promising divisions within the group

Careers in decentralized organizations are attractive to those who seek Status and Power/Influence. Middle management has considerable autonomy and is less rule-bound than in production organizations. However, since the units are fairly small, it's difficult to get any real experience of the overall operation. Analysts may acquire head office roles and get stuck there. In spite of any disadvantages, there is a direct connection with end results, so meaning is high.

Andrew is the financial director of Bulldog Intelligent Buildings Ltd. The parent company is Bulldog International Plc, which employs 98,000 people in 72 countries across the world. Andrew's company employs only 700 people and specializes in installing electronic devices for heat control and fire protection in buildings. Andrew's viewpoint of organizations was: 'We are a good business. We know our market and our product. We aim to be technological leaders in our game. BIB is managed by a board of directors and we have a lot of freedom to manage the way we want to. BI (the parent company) keep a very close eye on our figures. They are down on us like a dog on a rabbit if there are any signs of trouble. Otherwise we're left alone. Each year we present our strategies and forecasts at God's Palace (the headquarters building). We are small enough for everyone to know what we're all about.' This is typical of work in a decentralized organization.

5. 'ORGANIC' ORGANIZATIONS

The previous four kinds of organization are best suited to managing existing and largely predictable situations. When something dramatically new has to be done then an 'organic' organization is best. If what's needed is to build a new generation computer or to manage a rock and roll group, then the rather formal options that we've already discussed are inappropriate; a flexible team approach is necessary.

Innovation requires people to break away from established patterns; standardization or formalization stifle creativity and inhibit experiment. Innovation needs an organization that is anti-bureaucratic and co-ordinated by frequent meetings and *ad hoc* arrangements. Clear job demarcations, invariable routines and bureaucratic disciplines aren't helpful at all. All manner of communication techniques must be used to co-ordinate work, and change is often needed. A good example of an organic organization is NASA. In the first eight years of its life, this organization changed its structure seventeen times. And it did land men on the moon on schedule.

Organic organizations grow complex and untidy – often using complex managerial arrangements – yet this is essential to their innovative vitality. Employees, especially managers, develop skills in handling bewildering and divergent situations. They become expert co-ordinators and resource allocators. Power is held by those who have the expertise rather than by formal bosses. Top management has the key role of accumulating resources and re-assigning specialists to meet the needs of the moment. Strategy is reviewed many times as new facts emerge, and long-term planning may actually impede achievement since only the originators of ideas know what's needed to get the tasks done. Top managers spend much time identifying strategic options and clarifying broad aims. They strive to make choices on the basis of highly complex arguments and, although they try to control, they often find that they can only intervene after the event, when the money has already been spent.

Organizations of this type tend to be most dramatically creative in their youth. Later, bureaucracy usually creeps in and traditional organization forms usurp the organic model. The breeding ground of genuine innovation is often outside the established organization.

From the career viewpoint, such organizations are appropriate for those driven by Creativity and Autonomy. They don't suit people who are bureaucratic in attitude. Talents are very important and a high premium is placed on competence. High tolerance of change and turbulence is vital.

Simon is an electronic systems manager. He's in charge of a group of engineers who are devising new communications equipment for military use. He said: 'Basically my job is to apply brainpower to solve problems that no one has yet identified. We are a small team and no one is really the boss. I need to know what everyone is doing; we have a daily update meeting and apart from that we get together as and when it's necessary. There's a lot of talking and thinking out together. I work on the flip chart a lot. Sometimes we just sit about looking glum, since nobody can think of a way round the current problem. Then someone has a flash of inspiration, and we have an answer. Maybe it will work, maybe not. But we try it. Every now and again some berk from head office comes to monitor our performance, but he soon leaves because he just can't follow what's going on.' This is typical of work in an organic organization.

CONCLUSION

None of the respondents in the Richmond Survey had a theoretical grasp of organization design but they all experienced the realities described above.

The careerist should be able to choose which organizational environment is most congenial. When you know what suits you it is easier to make it happen.

Now complete the following Organizational Careers Analysis and use the data for later work in the book.

ORGANIZATIONAL CAREERS ANALYSIS

Answer the questions below at length and retain your answers for use in action planning later in this book.

1. What category of organization do you work for at present? (Tick as appropriate)
   - (a) Simple structure
   - (b) Large production organization
   - (c) Professional organization
   - (d) Decentralized organization
   - (e) Organic organization

2. What is your role at present? (Tick as appropriate)
   - (a) Operator
   - (b) Manager
   - (c) Analyst
   - (d) Support staff
   - (e) Director

3. How far does your current organization provide you with work experiences that you enjoy? (Give examples)

4. How far does your current organization offer career development possibilities that attract you? (Give examples)

5. What would you find attractive and unattractive about working in a 'simple structure'? (Refer to text to refresh your mind)

BENEFITS	DISADVANTAGES

6. What would you find attractive and unattractive about working in a 'large production organization'? (Refer to text to refresh your mind)

BENEFITS	DISADVANTAGES

7. What would you find attractive and unattractive about working in a 'professional organization'? (Refer to text to refresh your mind)

BENEFITS	DISADVANTAGES

8. What would you find attractive and unattractive about working in a 'decentralized organization'? (Refer to text to refresh your mind)

BENEFITS	DISADVANTAGES

9. What would you find attractive and unattractive about working in an 'organic organization'? (Refer to text to refresh your mind)

BENEFITS	DISADVANTAGES

You have completed your study of the ways in which organizations influence careers. Remember that your work experiences will be greatly affected by your choice of role and organizational type. The careerist will search for a congenial setting in which to express his or her drivers and talents. Remember, 'there's no place like home'.

STEP EIGHT

Where Should I Aim?

'For I dipt into the future, far as human eye could see,
Saw the Vision of the world, and all the wonder that would be.'
Tennyson

THE NEXT DECADE

It's time to start looking ahead. You have reflected on yourself from several viewpoints. You are clearer about your drivers, frustrations, achievements, talents, constraints, and the kind of organizational settings which suit you. Where do you go from here? Your acquisition of self-awareness will only be beneficial if it motivates you to take action.

In this section we invite you to paint a picture of what you want to become. I want you to create a 'vision of the future'. Your vision should be long-term, bold, speculative, and partly derived from your intuition. However, remember that the vision of the future must be cast in the real world of tomorrow. If it's going to be useful, it will have to be both achievable and desirable. Then it will inspire and direct you in the coming months and years.

Look through the job advertisements in any journal or newspaper. What do they ask for? Organizations want managing directors, security guards, rodent operatives or oboe players. They're trying to fill holes in their enterprises. Individual careerists offer their talents and drives, but organizations aren't interested in people as such; they're looking for solutions to their problems. A vision of your future career should not be a fantasy which ignores the market. Building a career requires that people define their path in a language which the world of work will understand.

The Richmond Survey suggested that those who 'envision' their careers from a marketing viewpoint gain considerable clarity. This needs some explanation. Marketing is the management discipline which orientates a business towards the world outside. It scrutinizes existing customers, categorizes them methodically, searches for potential customers, predicts their wants and needs, and assiduously evaluates competitors. Marketeers should be the intelligence department and commercial conscience of an organization. They define and help sustain a competitive advantage for the business they serve.

Marketing has a relatively short history. In 1960, Professor Theodore Levitt of the Harvard Business School published a paper entitled 'Marketing Myopia' in which he propounded that survival depends on doing everything necessary to satisfy the customer. Levitt introduced the concept of marketing to businessmen all over the world. Essentially, marketing says that the customer comes first. This is distinctly different from salesmanship, which is the craft of using stratagems in order to get people to buy a product.

All this is relevant to careerists in several ways. A careerist should consider herself or himself as a 'customer-creating' and 'customer-satisfying' organism. Every aspect of behaviour is relevant, right down to the way shoelaces are tied. Careerists should carefully study the real needs of the customer, not rely on their own assumptions. They should also avoid excessive dependence on short-term success, since it's much more important to provide long-term value.

Imagine that you hired a marketeer to consider *you* as a product. The first step is to investigate what your potentially saleable assets are. The marketeer would evaluate strengths, non-strengths and weaknesses, and then specify potential products or services. Good marketeers also put a lot of emphasis on detecting driving forces, which are flows of energy and commitment which mobilize effort.

John, the catering consultant, described how he came to realize the fundamental importance of looking outwards. He said: 'When I first started to market my consultancy services my attention was on my own thoughts and feelings. I was preoccupied with my nerves, my needs, my appearance and my dignity. Then someone pointed out that this was a bunch of crap. Prospective clients weren't interested in me. All they wanted was a good job done. I started to think about how I could be useful. This was a real turning point.' John had to build a bridge between himself and his clients. Careerists must do the same, but over a much longer timescale.

In order to begin to clarify your vision of the future it might seem desirable to begin with 'now'. In fact, most career books assume that this is the best thing to do. But rather than consider immediate market opportunities, respondents in the Richmond Survey taught me that we need to look at more distant horizons first. Careers are, by definition, half a lifetime long. They need an overall direction and purpose. Second (perhaps) only to marriage, your career is the longest project you'll ever undertake. If you don't have a long-term perspective, it's difficult to sculpt a meaningful career. Decisions taken for short-term reasons have long-lasting consequences.

A personal experience of mine demonstrates the point. On leaving university I became a trainee assistant film editor at the BBC, which is an entry point for a coveted career in television. After ten months I resigned, largely because, as a headstrong young graduate, I felt cheated spending my days labelling cans, listing numbers, running errands and keeping film off-cuts tidy. My decision was much more significant than I realized at the time. Today, I watch credits on TV productions and see that my ex-colleagues are now fully fledged directors and producers. The brutal fact is that my impulsive decision to resign effectively closed the door on a career in television. If I'd had a clearer vision of my future in television, those few early years as a film editor's handyman might have seemed like a small price to pay.

My experience was typical. Pondering over the transcripts of the Richmond Survey sample led me to believe that the proper time-horizon for careerists is ten years. Less than a decade gives inadequate time for fundamental initiatives to be made, while longer time frames are too remote and speculative.

The question becomes simple. What do you want to be doing a

decade from now? 'It may be simple,' I can hear you saying, 'but what a question!' As Zia pointed out in her first interview, 'I don't know where I'll be next week, let alone in a decade.' Well, relax; you won't have to answer the question precisely. But it is important to identify the kind of career that you're looking for in the longer term and then express your desire in language which the world of work understands.

A ten-year career horizon must be partly a work of fantasy. Who knows what will happen? So many unexpected and unpredictable events will occur that any vision of the future is likely to be incomplete. Yet it's surprising how many people achieve their long-term ambitions. The Richmond Survey had eleven people (20 per cent) who were working in roles which they'd determined before the age of sixteen.

A ten-year perspective must be a 'vision of the future'. This is essentially an inspired picture of what could be. Visions are not just logical extrapolations of present trends. They are novel formulations of possibility and intention which incorporate values, beliefs and intuitions. Yet a vision is not an ephemeral fantasy. Effective visions are inspired ideas rooted in practical possibility.

The idea of fashioning a career like a sculptor shapes a stone figure is helpful. A long time-horizon is needed because the basic shape must be determined early on. Perhaps the most common impediment to long-term career sculpting is the feeling expressed by Peter, who said: 'I'm not really sure what I want to do, so I just operate from day to day.' The lack of long-term direction deprives the individual of thrust and focus. Successful careerists assert that it is vital to prepare well to go somewhere.

This both shapes a career and develops the individual. You only learn how to achieve by achieving. People who neglect development during foundation phases of their careers, when the basic shape is moulded, are unlikely to catch up later. Accomplished individuals find it easier to refashion their careers in the light of personal or environmental changes.

For the careerist, the vision of the future is an essential tool. It focuses thought and provides coherence and purpose. Career visions don't come easily. They're emotionally based, and human emotions are notoriously impervious to logical thought. I've come to believe that a vision of the future must be discovered, not purchased. It emerges through reflection, creative thought and down-to-earth sense. After reading this chapter, you'll be asked to articulate your own long-term vision of the future. You will be asked to clarify the environments within which you want to work, the roles which you wish to play and the responsibilities that you wish to undertake. This must be done with an eye on the market.

Some people find that career visioning demands unaccustomed creativity, requiring them to escape from the limitations of their current thinking and gain totally new perspectives. Jerry felt that this was essential and described the process this way: 'My career was affected more than anything by a book which I bought in 1967. You won't believe it when I tell you the title. The book was *Tales of the Dervishes* and it's a collection of Sufi stories. One tale really hit me. Someone had lost a key one evening and was searching for it under the lamplight. In fact, he'd lost the key in a darker place but was looking where he could see best. I was struck by this. We all keep to familiar territory. I decided to try to be bold and question every assumption. If you turn a problem on its head, then there is usually a different way.'

Margret, who suffers from muscular dystrophy, amplified this point in a very personal way. She said, 'For me, life is about quality not merely quantity. I could see my life as a tragedy, but decided not to take that route. I've come to value the simple things in life like peace, beauty and companionship. I've learned gratitude. I step outside my selfish experience and look at things from a completely different perspective.' Such creativity is enriching and attractive. It provides the excitement in a vision of the future.

All of this is rather conceptual. What does it mean in practice? One of the most visionary careerists in the Richmond Survey was Ruth, a fifty-four-year-old actress. She had carefully weighed up her own strengths to thrive in a highly competitive environment. It is worth quoting part of the interview at some length:

Where Should I Aim?

Interviewer: What do you see as your marketable advantages?
Ruth: Look at me carefully.
Interviewer: Pardon?
Ruth: Take a good look at me and tell me what you see. Don't be shy.
Interviewer: Well, an attractive middle-aged woman.
Ruth: Would you like to take me away for a dirty weekend?
Interviewer: Pardon?
Ruth: Do you fancy me?
Interviewer: Frankly, no; but I can see that a few years ago I would have been scratching at your door.
Ruth: That's it. When I was in my twenties I just radiated sex appeal. They adored me. Then I began to sag here, spread there, and get a worn look. I sat down and thought about the future. Sex wouldn't last for ever, so I decided to learn to be an actress after ten years in the business.

Ruth went on to describe how she had predicted the growing influence of television and developed her skills as a character actress, taking great care not to become typecast. She took the action necessary to transform her vision of the future into reality.

Another practical illustration illustrates the principle. A couple are about to retire. They remember blissful holidays on the south coast and decide to live overlooking the sea. A cottage is purchased one bright spring day and the couple move from their established community with best wishes from old friends. Five years later the image of relaxed comfort in an idyllic landscape has been shattered. The cottage is damp, inconvenient and far from the shops. With age, and arthritic knees, the small hill from the village has become a daily torment. The local community remain unfriendly and friends rarely visit.

What has gone wrong? The couple did have a vision of the future (a cottage by the sea) but failed to fully test its reality. Many people could have given valuable advice but were not invited to do so. Predictable problems like hills and inhospitable communities were not foreseen. The vision was underdeveloped and undercritiqued.

It became a foolish talisman rather than the basis for a wise and progressive plan. Visions of the future need a firm foundation in reality.

Clarity about what you want is an important tool for personal strategy, and there is increasing support for the apparently absurd idea that 'willing' something makes it more likely to come about. Intention is an ingredient of success. The hypothesis is that if you want something badly enough, the possibility of your actually getting it is increased. Tony, a wealthy industrialist and a veritable fisherman of opportunities, said in his career interview: 'It's a process of gathering intentions. Once you know what you want, it becomes possible to start things going. Then opportunities begin to happen. The key skill is recognizing opportunities, and you only see these when you are hungry for them.'

The vision of the future is the primary tool for introducing meaning into careers. It integrates apparently disparate components and provides aims which are simple, stretching, desirable, and coherent. To use Tony's phrase, a vision of the future enables someone to 'gather intentions' and prepare for opportunity, advantage or setback.

CAREER VISIONS

A career vision of the future is partly a work of fantasy but should not be fantastic. There are five basic elements:

1. EXPLICIT ASSUMPTIONS

Assumptions are beliefs about what is good or bad, valid or invalid, worthwhile or worthless. They cannot be proved true or false, either because essential information isn't available or because matters of principle are involved. Assumptions have to be made about the external environment (e.g. the government will not abolish university grants) and the inner environment (e.g. I will be able to pass my examinations in architecture).

Both internal and external assumptions which influence your career need to be expressed, and tested for their logical coherence and realism. This is often practically possible. Richard, now a Church of England priest, made the following fascinating comments:

Interviewer: You were working as a draughtsman and decided to make a career change.

Richard: Yes. But it didn't come easily. In the drawing office I began to see myself as a man without a true purpose. I felt that I was spending my time without contributing anything real to the world. I started to see everything in terms of a struggle between the forces of light and the forces of darkness. This might seem bizarre. I became convinced that I had a vocation, and started to talk to people about how I saw things. I wanted to expose my thinking and see whether I believed what I was saying. I wanted to listen to myself.

Interviewer: So you had many conversations.

Richard: Yes. Many were significant. The picture was coloured-in slowly. One conversation stands out. I was talking to my doctor in the pub one evening and he asked, 'What do you believe is important, in five simple sentences with no long words?' I told him, and he challenged me on each point. It was a baptism of fire. At the end of that conversation I knew where I stood.

2. DETAILED PROPOSALS

Effective visions of the future are more like architects' models than two-dimensional paintings. They should be refined from a rough sketch into a three-dimensional model which demonstrates that practical problems have been solved, at least in miniature. An effective vision of the future will have been thought through in considerable detail. Mary's career interview demonstrated this well:

Interviewer: You were a civil servant and decided to change. How did you think this through?

Mary: Yes, I had to take the 7.56 train every morning. But I knew I wanted something different and felt a great attraction to working with children. Through voluntary work I had met Dr Zedenburg, who is a remarkable man. He uses what's almost a sixth sense to communicate with the deaf. He has learned how to extend their other senses and help deaf people relate more fully to others. I wanted to become a student in his clinic, but I really had to think it through. Where would I live? How much money would I have? How would I feel about the loss of status? How would I feel about the insecurity? Was this my thing?

Interviewer: What did you do to work all this out?

Mary: I wrote an essay, like we did at school, called 'Starting Afresh'. This was as accurate a picture of how life would be if I joined Dr Zedenburg as I could devise. Two weeks later I read it again and handed in my notice to the civil service. The essay showed me what I wanted and that it was feasible.

Useful visions are capable of being fully articulated. This is an essential test for ensuring that the vision is not paltry or superficial. Underdeveloped visions are a major hazard since they give an illusion of direction without the depth necessary for sagacious decision-making. Robert, an out-of-work shop owner, provided a good illustration of the importance of full articulation of a vision. Here's a short extract from his career interview:

Interviewer: How did you decide to buy the shop?

Robert (looking down and folding his arms): Well, in retrospect, I didn't give it enough thought. I was in this pub, and there was someone I knew vaguely with a pocketful of twenties. He was sitting buying rounds and he had that air of someone who didn't have to rush, know what I mean? He owned a shop, and I suppose I thought that could be me. After that I plunged in.

Interviewer: An unwise decision?

Robert: Half-cocked, more like. I just hadn't realized what I was letting myself in for.

Robert's case is a rather extreme example of the lack of a fully articulated career vision, which is a common phenomenon. Careerists who want to hang on to pie-in-the-sky dreams rather than expose their thinking to rational analysis are taking big risks with their future.

3. EXCITING IMAGES

Useful visions of the future are optimistic and heartening. A dour and pessimistic view of what's ahead is a constraint. This has happened to Alison, who said: 'I see the future with considerable trepidation. My whole life is conditioned by decisions that were taken for me when I was fourteen years old. I came from a medical family and it was natural for me to enter nursing. The job is all-demanding. I feel a desire to spread my wings and broaden my mind. I'd like to stop the world for a while. But it can't happen. I'm committed financially and morally. This is my way of life, damn it.'

A vision of the future which includes hope and progression gives most advantage to the careerist. It provides a channel for the expression of emotions charged with positive energy. These are inherently enlivening and encouraging. Jerry, a wealthy entrepreneur, was aware of the value of exciting visions:

Interviewer: How do you go about deciding to commit yourself to a new venture?

Jerry: It's partly at gut level. I see what turns me on. I ruminate on a proposal to see how I feel about it. I want to get a splurge of excitement. We are wiser than we know. I can feel if something is good.

Interviewer: Is it largely a question of 'feel'?

Jerry: Initially, yes, but then I put the ideas through my 'Mastermind Test'. I critique a thing to death. I knock it from every angle. I'm careful not to rig the test. If the idea stands up to punishment, then – and only then – will I think about it seriously.

Interviewer: So it's a combination of heart and mind.

Jerry: Exactly, but there's one more ingredient. I call it 'attraction power'. I might believe in something but still not be interested. I have to feel attracted to something, and drawn to being involved. That tells me that it's right.

4. REALISTIC AIMS

Effective visions of the future cannot be totally inconceivable. The author of this book may become a writer, politician or a university professor. He will not become a model for shampoo advertisements (little hair), an athlete (few muscles) or a whisky blender (poor sense of smell).

There's a logical dilemma here. If a vision of the future is what could happen, then how can it be tested for reality since in theory anything could happen? The answer is 'Quite. But . . .' Consider your author sitting in a field and having his pate licked by a cow. This results, by some magical process, in new hair growing. Then, perhaps, he might become a male model for shampoo advertisements. However, the probabilities of this happening are slight. Everything may be possible, but everyday experience tells us that some things are miracles rather than achievable aims. The wise careerist will not base his or her future on the assumption that there will be a plentiful supply of miracles.

Testing visions of the future for reality requires evaluation of probabilities. Archie, a freelance writer, described the interesting process by which he did this:

Interviewer: You were a university lecturer in biophysics.

Archie: Yes. But I had a yearning to do something different. I had the freedom to start again.

Interviewer: So what did you do?

Archie: I thought about what I wanted and a lifestyle that suited me. I thought about those times in my life when I was really content. There were three scenarios which appealed.

Interviewer: Three different options?

Archie: Yes. I could become a consultant, a photographer or a writer. Each was possible but after a lot of thought I discarded photography because it's such an overcrowded profession. Writing appealed and I believed that I could become a technical journalist. So I decided to test myself and write part-time for a year.

Interviewer: What was the result?

Archie: Encouraging. My work was published. I was paid. I enjoyed the work. I began to feel more like a swan. Writing became a practical possibility.

5. FIRM PRINCIPLES

A career vision of the future is a comprehensive personal statement which captures what you want to happen in your life. Inevitably, visions are concerned with beliefs and values. How can you identify where you want to go if you do not know what is worthwhile?

The most helpful vision statements have a moral quality. This was put clearly by Caroline in her interview. She said, 'I have always wanted to be more admirable than admired. I am prepared to sacrifice some of my life to expediency but, in the end, it's vital for me to do what I believe in. The quality of life is enhanced by art and by being in everyday contact with beautiful things. I couldn't prove this, but I believe it. So, it was easy for me to work at making this happen for real.'

Caroline found that her values were the mainspring of her vision. She sought ways to transform a set of beliefs into action. In fact, she had discovered the principles of a counselling approach known as 'values clarification'. This provides a useful checklist for validating values.

A vision of the future should meet these seven criteria:

1. It is freely chosen
2. It has been chosen from alternatives

3. The consequences of each alternative have been evaluated (this demonstrates thought)
4. It's prized and feels 'good' (this demonstrates respect for the value)
5. You're proud of it and will tell others
6. You're prepared to act to implement your vision
7. It fits into your total life pattern

FINDING YOUR TEN-YEAR CAREER VISION

Since work is such a significant part of life, the question 'How do I want my career to develop?' isn't very different from the age-old question 'Who am I?' This search has concerned mystics, great teachers and ordinary men and women through the ages. No fundamental insights are going to be given here, but some practical suggestions gathered from careerists' experience.

The career histories of members of the Richmond Survey sample showed that it was vital to spend time developing a ten-year vision of the future. This means that you should obey the six 'golden rules':

Rule One – Seek to trust yourself

There is an inner monitor which gives the individual important intuitive information on what he or she should do. If this voice can be heard and trusted, it provides much useful guidance.

Rule Two – Keep yourself open to new experiences

Those who felt that their careers were progressive insisted that they had to keep themselves open to new experiences. It's impossible to predict what will be significant or meaningful. We're perpetually being bombarded with new inputs. A willingness to respond to the moment is as valuable as diligent planning.

Where Should I Aim?

Rule Three – Be cautious about who you serve

Careers are personal journeys, yet there's always a temptation to serve others and neglect self-interest for the actual or perceived good of another.

Rule Four – Find ways to be truly authentic

The strongest careers are those in which the person is fully involved. There is no game or pretence. Everything that reduces authenticity erodes energy and debilitates the person.

Rule Five – Enjoy travelling, not just arriving

Careers are a continual process of change. Satisfaction is gained through enjoying the experience rather than just the end state.

Rule Six – Take care not to burn out

Keep healthy. Don't exhaust yourself. Each day will demand more from you.

A ten-year career vision gives the careerist a target to aim towards. To summarize, these are the primary ingredients:

- Concern with the marketplace
- Long-term perspective
- Creative thinking
- Deep reflection on values and principles
- Thorough consideration of risk and realism
- Well-considered assumptions
- Detailed comprehensive proposals
- A sense of excitement about the outcome
- Genuine and honest reflection
- A continuing willingness to be open to experience

Now complete the following project, as described. Allow yourself ample time to mull over the whole issue of your long-term career future. This should be a reflective, not hurried, review. Many people find it helpful to spend some time alone for quiet contemplation. Look over the project and plan how you can best undertake it. Be willing to return to this step time and time again over the coming months.

VISION OF YOUR CAREER FUTURE

Stage One – Visioning the Future

Answer the seven questions below. Allow yourself to reflect at length before you reply. Use a pencil to record your comments and be willing to amend or change frequently.

1. What ten possibilities come to mind as long-term careers for me?

    1.

    2.

    3.

    4.

    5.

    6.

    7.

    8.

    9.

    10.

2. Which of these do I really like?

    1.

    2.

    3.

    4.

    5.

3. What are the aspects that appeal to me?

Appealing aspects	Why?

4. What are the constraints on my freedom of choice?

Constraints	How?

5. Look at your answers to the first four questions and select a vision of your career future that is clear, meaningful and achievable. Write a 100-word description below (do not write less).

6. How can I get others involved to fully understand my vision?

Who?	How?

7. Do I have other aims which may conflict?

Other aims	Kind of conflicts?

This is an outline statement of your 'vision of the future'. Allow yourself time for contemplation. Use your emotions as well as your intellect to help you. When you feel clear about where you are going you are ready to proceed to stage two.

Stage Two – Validating Your Vision

Over the last twenty years business leaders have become increasingly aware of the importance of 'marketing'. This management discipline enables companies to decide what goods or services will stand the best chance of sustaining a continuing competitive advantage.

Careerists benefit from seeing themselves as 'products' and undertaking a similar analysis using established marketing techniques.

Answer the three questions below in the space provided (to force you to be pithy). Use a notepad to prepare your answers.

Unless you are very confident, it is best to write in pencil and have an eraser handy.

SELF-MARKETING STUDY

1. Each of us has talents, skills, knowledge, resources etc. that someone else may wish to buy. These are our 'marketable attributes' or MAs. Reflect on your earlier visioning and list your current MAs in order of your evaluation of their attractiveness to potential employers/users.

   (i)

   (ii)

   (iii)

   (iv)

   (v)

2. Now you must think about your 'competitors'. These are other groups, people or mechanical/electronic systems which can also provide what you wish to offer.

(a) List the actual competitors you face today and rate the competition as very weak, weak, medium, strong, or very strong.

Competitors	Strength
(i)	vw w m s vs
(ii)	vw w m s vs
(iii)	vw w m s vs
(iv)	vw w m s vs
(v)	vw w m s vs

(b) Think about the likely changes in your competitors in the next ten years. What new factors may influence their strength or weakness?

Competitors	Likely changes over 10 years
(i)	
(ii)	
(iii)	
(iv)	
(v)	

3. Now consider what efforts you are making to develop new marketable assets which will assist you to transform your vision of the future into reality.

(a) What new marketable attributes are you trying to acquire now?

(i)

(ii)

(iii)

(b) What new marketable attributes do you have plans to acquire in the next two years?

(i)

(ii)

(iii)

(c) What percentage of your time are you currently investing in developing new marketable attributes?

——— %

This concludes the project. Look back over your answers. Do you feel clearer? If not, think again. When you feel ready, proceed to Step Nine.

STEP NINE

What Are My Objectives?

'You can never plan the future by the past.'
Burke

THIS YEAR'S PLAN

'The net is closing,' as fishermen say. After a lot of exploration, you're clearer now about your vision of the future. The next phase is to transform this strategic insight into action, and to develop concrete objectives so that you can move from your current position to where you want to go.

A comparison will help you to see what Step Nine is all about. Set the scene in your mind: war generals are sitting in map-rooms planning their strategies, moving their armies around like pieces in some gigantic game of chess. They create long-range scenarios and evaluate risks. Meanwhile, somewhere on the battlefield a platoon of men is pinned down in a ditch considering how to advance to the crest of the next hill, where a well-protected machine-gun nest dominates the valley.

In Step Nine we're concerned with the men in the ditch. Those short-term advances are a vital part of your wider career strategy. Let's assume that you've already defined your career aims. (What? You haven't? Well, go back to Step Eight and work through it again!) Now you need to acquire enough clarity and precision to transform your broad aims into concrete objectives. Those of you who read detective stories at bedtime have an advantage here. You'll know that great sleuths solve apparently inexplicable crimes with careful study and just a pinch of inspiration. Careerists need exactly the same attention to detail.

In spite of the fact that setting objectives has been the major management tool of the last twenty years, it still isn't well understood. And since you need to understand it, I'm going to give you a short lecture. An objective is a unique tool. It's a bridge between meaning and doing. Objectives grasp aspirations and transform them into the raw material for plans. They define what's important or unimportant, and they enable us to focus our endeavours towards achievement. An objective is the primary tool for galvanizing human effort to achieve specific results.

Objective-setting is often done badly. People prefer to get into action (which is concrete and exciting), rather than devote efforts to clarifying objectives (which are often abstract). As one careerist put it: 'Objective-setting makes my brain hurt.'

We can't set objectives in a vacuum. Since objectives direct our attention towards solving problems or seizing opportunities, this requires that you have 'tuned in' to your needs, wants and constraints, and discovered what needs attention. The first half of *Managing Your Own Career* is designed to help you do this.

Objectives should address the key issues which face your career at the moment. We categorize these by: importance (will solving this problem or seizing this opportunity make a difference?); by type (what kind of challenge does this present?); and by urgency (will the problem get worse or the opportunity go away if it isn't tackled soon?). Once we've identified key issues, we can set priorities so that we focus on the most serious and urgent requirements first.

Objectives need to be realistic. Stephan, a journalist, was one of the respondents who had a very high opinion of his own talent:

Stephan: Really I should be on Fleet Street by now. I've got the talent and the experience but I'm too unconventional for them. They don't recognize a visionary voice. People won't hear my message that they should open their hearts to new experiences.

Interviewer: What are your career objectives for the next year?

Stephan: I intend to make a very considerable impact on the media world.
Interviewer: Can you put this more precisely?
Stephan: It's not like that. It's inspirational. I will get people to listen. The medium will come. It's others who must recognize me.

Stephan continued in the same vein, enlarging on his ideas for making a huge impact, before leaving this interview late to cover a council meeting in a London borough. His objectives were vague flights of fancy, not at all rooted in the real world.

Some objectives are expressed in very broad terms; for example, 'to be a successful doctor'. Others are specific; for example, 'to become proficient at treating bunions'. Broad career objectives are useful because they provide a general overview, liberating imagination and helping us to explore the full range of options available. However, broad objectives do not enable us to establish precisely what needs to be done; we need specific career objectives for that.

If you have a broad career objective and you want to formulate a plan and establish specific objectives, this is what you should do. Write the broad objective on the top of a sheet of paper and then ask yourself the question: 'How will I achieve this?' Generate as many options as you can, and express these as objectives. Record all the objectives. Are they specific enough now to provide the help you need? If not, take each and ask the question again: 'How will I achieve this?' You'll eventually find that what emerges is a network of objectives in the shape of a pyramid. At the top is the broad career objective, and at the base of the pyramid is the myriad of specific objectives which lead directly to definite action programmes.

Page 215 has an example of a simple pyramid of objectives. You can see that the four specific objectives at the bottom of the pyramid are practical, whereas the broad objective at the top (to extend my management experience) is far too vague to be useful; it is a New Year's resolution, not a tool for effective self-management.

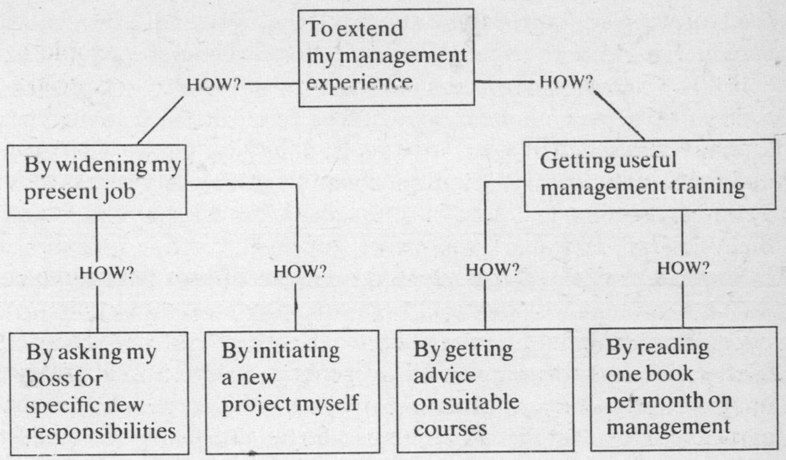

There are two kinds of objectives. 'Output' objectives state what should be achieved in measurable terms. 'Competence' objectives are less well understood but equally important. They answer the question: 'What do I need to be *good at* in order to achieve my output objectives?' Output and competence objectives go hand in hand, supporting each other. An example helps to explain this important distinction. Ruth, the actress, set herself an output objective which was to act in two major television plays next year. This could only be achieved if her acting was exciting and reliable. To be an exciting and reliable actress were her competence objectives.

Objective-setting is almost complete when you have a full and clear definition of what you are seeking to achieve in the short term. But let me introduce you to another helpful piece of jargon. One thing that should be built into any plan to achieve an objective is a 'success measure'. Although people seem to dislike measuring rods to guide their activities, successful careerists emphasize that measurement is essential.

It's obvious when you think about it. How can you judge success without a technique for measuring it? It's sometimes easy to see how effectiveness can be measured: Jack now runs a shop with four assistants and he evaluates his overall performance by studying the weekly takings. However, he decided he wanted to improve customer relations. He puzzled about how he could assess this objective, and said: 'I was in a quandary. How could I measure whether staff politeness was being improved?' After reflection, Jack decided to interview a random sample of twenty customers each month, and ask them to rate the quality of service in his shop. He stood self-consciously at the door with a clipboard and gathered feedback about the 'politeness level' of his staff. He found it helpful to 'put the results of the monthly surveys on a graph. The information was really useful. The staff took the whole thing very seriously and we bumped up the takings by 11 per cent in six months.'

Jack couldn't have achieved this if he hadn't asked himself this question: 'How am I going to measure achievement so that I can objectively judge performance?' Only when he could monitor performance could he take appropriate action. Career objectives can also be measurable. People need to establish their own criteria for success and find ways to monitor their progress. Without this they lack the 'helicopter' viewpoint.

It's useful to cast objectives within a time frame. A start date and a finish date, like the imminent threat of hanging, do concentrate the mind. As the submission date for this manuscript drew nearer, I began to start working before dawn. A realistic time frame, which includes a 'Murphy factor', is a useful aid.

People find that one set of objectives will often conflict with others. This was well illustrated by the career interview with Tim, the doctor.

Interviewer: What are your immediate career objectives?

Tim: I have three: to earn a lot of money, to settle down and to study some more.

Interviewer: Are these objectives compatible with each other?

Tim: Absolutely not. To make money I should go back to Saudi. To settle down I should stay here. To study would cost me thousands.

Interviewer: How do you cope with the conflict between your objectives?

Tim: Two ways. I give them priorities and then I question how I feel. I want my heart to be in my choice. I refer back to my overall life plan.

Tim had found a formula to balance the relative merits of different objectives. This is essentially a question of values and priorities. Your vision of the future, which is the foundation of career aims, provides the criteria for making such judgements.

Objectives are best treated as targets, not as inflexible manacles. The unexpected does happen. James was an accountant with a multinational food company where he ran a department devoted to meeting the bureaucratic needs of a carefully structured monolithic conglomerate. While rambling in the Black Mountains of Wales, he stopped for lunch at a small pub and fell into conversation with a hiker. They talked, and it emerged that the other man was an entrepreneur who had recently launched a new range of biotech products. Two hours later, after the fifth pint, the entrepreneur suggested, 'Why don't you come and have a look at my new company. See if we still get on when we are sober. If we like each other I'd like you to join me as Commercial Director. We'll have a lot of fun, plenty of ups and downs, and maybe make our fortune.' A month later, with much anxiety, James handed in his resignation to the big company for which he worked, gave up his company car, and moved to the insecurity and excitement of a small new business.

James's case illustrates that sometimes good opportunities just seem to fall out of the sky. Unimaginable chains of events occur. But it would be foolish to rely on chance to guide our careers. Objectives always have a part to play. Although an incredible number of events shaped the careers of the Richmond Survey respondents, almost everyone found it possible to set objectives which allowed them to be open to opportunities. Simon, an electronics engineer, set himself an objective of entering technical management within a year. He joined a British Institute of Management working party studying hi-tech organizations. This brought him into contact with many managers and he began to understand how they think and operate. Several months later he was offered a technical management position. From one point of view this was a lucky break. But it had been worked for. The ground had been well prepared and seeds had been sown; the objective was met.

Career objectives have to be set in context. They must suit both the individual and the wider environment. Change is sometimes counter-productive. Mary, for example, will continue her studies in communication skills among deaf children this year. Others need to move on, either by expanding in their current role or finding a new job. Frank said: 'This is my year for a stunning change. I need a bigger job soon. I'm ready now and I don't want to go off the boil.'

For most careerists there comes a time to set an objective to change jobs, either within or outside their current organization. This is usually stressful, and sometimes traumatic. In the 1980s, human labour is less attractive than it has been at any other time since the depression of the 1930s. In spite of the inhospitable job market, approximately 6 million people change their jobs each year in Britain. The pattern is the same in other countries. One recent study demonstrated that about 40 million Americans are trying to change their employer at any given moment. But despite the fact that millions of people want different jobs, the employment scene is largely unregulated, unfair and unreasonable. It may not be a jungle, but it is certainly a heavily overgrown woodland.

The Richmond Survey confirmed the conclusions of other studies that people in the West often build careers by roundabout and unsystematic routes. Communist and socialist societies like the USSR try to control the movement of labour by central decree. For example, at one time a girl in Leningrad was identified as a future engineer for Siberia by the state bureaucracy. Her training would start immediately, and six years later she would be sitting on the Trans-Siberian Express on her way to start a new life. At least that was the theory. Whether it's the right way to do things is quite another question! The stance taken by Western capitalist societies is completely different. Regulation in job-finding is minimal. Those who want to employ people must go and find them. When people are deemed unsuitable or unnecessary they are expelled. It's a largely free market for both employer and employee. Attempts are sometimes made to set up a process to fit square pegs into square holes but a fully developed system does not exist. Responsibility for employment is delegated to the wide variety of labour users, so there can never be a totally regulated system for employment in a capitalist society.

Employers are largely motivated by self-interest. They want people to make their systems work and to solve problems. In fact, many employers feel ambivalent about having to employ people at all, since they're seen as potentially unreliable and troublesome. Far better, so many managers think, to have machines which are predictable and faithful. Of course, some managers act from a basis of principle, seeing work as a contribution to human community, but not even the compassionate can fight the logic of competition. As national employment trends show, employers will reduce their headcount if it increases profitability. Alan, a managing director, put it succinctly: 'I'm here to keep the chairman happy, and the only thing that brings a smile to his lips is profit.'

Bosses are not the only ones motivated by self-interest. Employees also seek the best for themselves. None of the fifty-three respondents in the Richmond Survey felt that loyalty played more than a marginal role in their career decision-making. Frank, working for an electronics company, said: 'I see myself as a moral mercenary. I'll play a tune as long as I'm paid well. My loyalties are firstly to myself and my family, then to my profession, and lastly to my paymaster.'

Not everyone will have short-term objectives to change their career paths. May, a teacher, went through a protracted re-evaluation of her career. She considered many options and finally decided that her present work entirely suited her. In spite of stressful classes and poor material rewards, her heart was in teaching. She decided to redouble her efforts to exploit her current job.

More commonly, people look for change. This may be cosmetic or revolutionary. The technology for making changes with maximum effectiveness and minimum risk is called 'management'. In this section we begin to apply part of the art and science of management to career development by setting career objectives .

How can someone work 'intelligently' on their career? Even experienced managers find it difficult to use their professional skills on themselves. Some months after his interview, I received a telephone call from William, a senior production manager in a complex chemical process plant. He was anxious and distressed. The job wasn't going well. William's plant had been dogged by production problems which, he felt, were 'matters completely outside my control'. He told me: 'The parent company was looking for blood to be spilt, and the blood had to be mine.' In effect, he was being moved from his current position into a more junior role; a very serious matter for a proud man of thirty-eight who had three children.

A counselling session followed. William was under a great deal of strain; he was full of bitterness, self-defensiveness, apprehension, and uncertainty. But the jungle fighter's instinct, telling him to behave wisely, was there too. We discussed the situation and he departed with an action list, with the first item being 'Manage myself like a pro'. William realized that management expertise was his most precious asset. Perhaps surprisingly, he hadn't seen his career problems as essentially managerial.

If managers are doing their jobs properly, they begin by clarifying broad aims which combine into a coherent vision of the future. We've already done that, in Step Eight. Then they embark on a systematic process to set objectives and establish the criteria by which they can measure success. This is the managerial logic that William found he had to use on his own career.

It's time to sit down and think about your short-term career objectives. A format for doing this is suggested in Your Career Objectives, the project on page 222. Before you begin it's worthwhile being 100 per cent clear about what a useful objective looks like. There are ten golden rules:

1. Objectives should be stated in specific terms.
2. Broad objectives should be logically extended into specific objectives.
3. You should be able to measure your degree of success in achieving your objectives.
4. Objectives should be reasonably achievable, not wild flights of fancy.
5. Objectives should be meaningful to you and consistent with your values and aims.
6. Give each objective a time frame for achievement which is stretching but not impossible.
7. Identify the competence objectives implicit in your output objectives, so you know what you have to be good at.
8. Bear the environment in mind so that your objectives are based in the real world.
9. Identify the relative importance of different objectives and weigh one against another to set priorities.
10. Be simple: three profound objectives are infinitely better than thirty trivial ones.

YOUR CAREER OBJECTIVES

This project helps you clarify your objectives through specific and measurable statements of what you want to achieve in the immediate future. It will not be easy to set career objectives as many imponderables always seem to intervene. Yet it is most important to be as precise and realistic as possible.

Begin this project only after you have carefully read Step Nine. Then complete the twelve items below in pencil. Discuss and reflect on the results. Only when you are happy with the output should you complete the project in ink to symbolize your own commitment to the outcome.

1. My long-range career aims are (refer to Step Eight, page 206):

2. This means that in the next twelve months my objectives could be (brainstorm a list):

3. Look at the objectives you have just generated. Categorize these according to 'realism' on a one to ten scale. Order your objectives with those you have the best chance of achieving at the top:

4. Select from the list in item 3 no more than four career objectives that you both wish to and probably can achieve in the next twelve months:

5. On this day next year the following differences in my work life will be apparent:

6. The likely difficulties I face in achieving my twelve months' objectives are:

7. In order to achieve my objectives I should acquire these new competencies or strengths:

8. I would like to get the help of others in achieving my objectives in the following ways:

9. I will take the following steps to validate the realism of my objectives:

10. I could measure my degree of success in achieving my objectives in the following ways:

11. My career objectives might conflict with other objectives in my life in these ways:

12. The objectives I set for the next year carry the following risks to me or my family:

You have established 'draft' career objectives for the next year. Reflect on your comments. Do your objectives seem feasible? Desirable? Stretching? Progressive? Allow yourself to mull over your analysis. Obtain feedback and comment from colleagues, friends and, perhaps, professional advisers.

Take your short-term objectives seriously. Work for precision. After several days' consideration finalize your objectives and write them in in ink. These should become a firm personal commitment.

STEP TEN

How Should I Develop Myself?

'Unto every one that hath shall be given.'
St Matthew

BUILDING COMPETENCE

The easiest way of building a progressive career is to be offered a succession of desirable opportunities. Obviously, people who are wanted are in a much better position than those who are not. Bob put it well when he said: 'The trick is to be right for promotion. I prefer to have someone twisting my arm and forcing me to take a better job.' There is an unequivocal link between career development and high competence. To some extent the cream does rise to the top of the milk!

High competence is not an abstract quality. It's related to performance in specific roles. Playing the oboe in a orchestra clearly requires different competencies from those needed to be an effective army officer.

Competence is the capacity to perform reliably to an acceptable standard. It is 'developed potential'. A simple analogy helps to explain the concept. You, the reader, can probably drive a car. At the moment you are reading, and not (hopefully) driving. Yet you have the intellectual, emotional and physical skills, knowledge, attitude, perceptual sharpness and willingness to drive. You possess everything needed to get behind the wheel and be fully responsible for the vehicle. You are a 'competent' driver.

Competence is not a simple concept. It has five components:

- Skill: being able to perform, in the correct sequence, difficult or complex techniques
- Knowledge: having relevant data, helpfully organized, and being able to use an appropriate body of knowledge
- Attitude: constructive emotional stance and willingness to perform to a high standard
- Self-concept: confidence in one's ability to achieve
- Perceptual sharpness: being able to pay attention to things that really matter in doing a good job

All five components interact, although one is sometimes pre-eminent. Knowledge is needed for skill, which guides perception, which shapes attitude and so on. Imagine it as a spider's web: thinking, feeling and performing all support each other to provide a competence. (I acknowledge the help given by Richard Boyatzis' book *The Competent Manager*, Wiley, New York 1982, in developing these concepts.)

All roles demand a number of specific competencies. Consider a driver again. He or she must drive the car safely, deal with minor mechanical emergencies, keep it insured and so on. Each of these activities makes different demands and requires distinct competencies. It's helpful to specify them for assessment and training. When you're driving in traffic correct road-positioning, judging road conditions and so on will need to be looked at separately.

In a fair world, people either acquire new roles because they already possess the necessary competencies, or because someone with power to make decisions about the careers of others believes that they can efficiently acquire them. The successful candidate is the one who appears to be the best bet for the job. Inevitably, judgements about potential performances are partly acts of faith since new job-holders will be asked to do things that they haven't done before.

If your career plan includes a change, then personal growth is required for you to acquire the necessary new competencies. It's unwise to rely on short cuts or gimmicks. Those who want a progressive career have three personal development assignments:

1. To be fully competent to perform the next job if at all possible
2. To demonstrate to 'selectors' that you possess the necessary competencies
3. To be able to acquire new competencies quickly

I analysed the Richmond Survey career biographies carefully and came to the firm conclusion that possession of relevant competencies was all-important. Making a career move by subterfuge or nepotism was hazardous, as absence of necessary competencies did not remain unnoticed. Harvey, now a redundant manager, was a tall, volatile man. He had been a consultant for several years before becoming a senior manager in a government welfare agency. His poor time management, his inability to formulate policy and his incompetence as team leader quickly became apparent and he was 'removed' after only five months in the job. He lacked the core competencies to handle the job, to the detriment of himself, his family, his employer, his subordinates and clients.

Developing competence is a long-term project. Earlier we compared career management to gardening. Good husbandry over many years is required, since very little can be achieved by a spurt of effort followed by months or years of neglect. Constant upgrading and maintenance of your competencies is required, as well as occasional big decisions which will enable you to acquire a new clutch of competencies.

The acquisition of new competencies is particularly important in key career changes. People sometimes find that there is an apparently unbridgeable chasm between their present position and where they want to be. When this happens the individual must search for a bridge. Without a way to cross the chasm, the seeker is condemned to walk along the edge looking for ways to escape.

How Should I Develop Myself?

Competencies are bridges: they enable a person to cross to where they want to be.

A typical career requires the development of new competencies which relate to predictable transitions throughout adult life. These are the key transitions for a careerist:

- School to college (theme: educational depth)
- College to work (theme: field of involvement)
- Work to expertise (theme: specialization)
- Expertise to power (theme: eminence)
- Power to ceiling (theme: levelling off)
- Ceiling to retirement (theme: lifestyle choice and decline)

In each transition the person faces new dilemmas and opportunities which are unlike anything previously experienced. It's important to prepare in advance for future transitions. Each presents a challenge of personal development.

The implication is that we must continue to learn and develop throughout our lives. Transitions occur perhaps once a decade and cannot be prevented. Although people may ignore or attempt to evade the next transition, the logic of biological ageing and contingent change of career focus is inexorable.

The scope and nature of new competencies which must be acquired throughout a career varies according to gender, occupation, social class and amount of social mobility. For example, women may transfer from work into family life and then back into work. This can require a lot of new learning. A few people may virtually escape acquiring new competencies. One person did this by becoming a groundsman when he was fifteen years old and remaining in this occupation until the age of seventy-one.

Sometimes unexpected transitions, like illness or redundancy, are imposed without warning and new competencies are suddenly required to cope with a previously unknown situation. Those who say that they have been successful in managing unexpected transitions report that they:

- Had sufficient wealth to cope with disturbances
- Took time off to contemplate their lives
- Discussed their situation carefully with others
- Were prepared to receive professional counselling
- Learned about transitions and related the ideas to themselves
- Had the warm support of others
- Carefully identified what new competencies were needed
- Took initiatives to get training
- Were prepared to be bold

Those careerists who rated themselves as 'unsuccessful' did not tend to think about developing new competencies. Instead they acted as if making a transition was like finding the magic door into a secret garden, often asking: 'How can I get people to take notice of me?' It usually emerged that the questioner made an implicit assumption that credibility can be acquired by stealth or trick. In fact, the only sound way to gain credibility is by becoming more able; respect can only be demanded after this has happened. Those who seek to raise their stature in the eyes of others find it more fruitful to ask: 'How can I gain more competence?'

Competency analysis is a superb practical tool for careerists. If you want to acquire a more senior or a different kind of job, begin by studying the people who succeed in the role at present. Ask yourself: What are their strengths? How do they approach their roles? What techniques do they use? How do they spend their time? When you have clearly identified the competencies of those performing the job you desire, examine your own capacities and ask yourself the question: Where am I lacking?

Understanding the competencies which are necessary for high performance in your next role provides an agenda for self-development. There's no need to copy all those who hold desired roles. That could be a recipe for disaster! The present job-holder may be incompetent and to model yourself on a poor performer would be lunacy. Study the way that high performers operate. Identify what he or she does well and learn to do it yourself.

Despite the importance of being prepared to handle the next job, people can and must take calculated risks, otherwise it would be impossible to grow. Every new prime minister is unproven; the incumbent grows by doing the job. However, risks should be minimized. Existing competence plus a systematic plan for overcoming areas of inadequacy is the best insurance for job retention and further career development.

Careerists are well advised to perform to an outstanding level in their current job, and then to try hard to ensure that they are recognized. To do this it's particularly important to acquire the framework of perception and thinking to the target job-holders. Alan said wisely: 'I wish to be able to predict what the boss is likely to say or do in all important particular situations. Reliably predicting what someone will do demonstrates that I am the master of their thinking patterns.'

We have already made the point in Step Four that jobs confine their holders. For this reason new competencies, especially those which require skill development, are difficult to acquire. For example, Arthur, an electronics engineer, led a small team of professionals but wanted to develop into general management. He was a delightful man who enjoyed music and solving technical problems and always told the unvarnished truth, without guile or pretension. However, he lacked the ability to lead in anything other than a 'participative' style. His career objective meant that he would have to acquire management skills which entailed a strong 'telling' style of leadership. Arthur recognized his lack of leadership strength but could not find a way of filling the gap since he didn't need to use a strongly directive leadership style for his present job. How was he to acquire the necessary new competence? After discussion a solution emerged: he would become a volunteer youth leader in his village. Later, as he undertook responsibility for wild and headstrong teenagers, Arthur developed an assertiveness and solidity of character that he could not have acquired through intellectual appreciation. He needed the experience of leading a wayward group of troublesome but basically constructive young people. In the next year Arthur gained a bundle of new leadership competencies which gave him a new strength of purpose and confidence that others found remarkable. This resulted in him being offered the career move he wanted.

Arthur's experience showed how hard it is to acquire competencies outside your present job. Betty had a similar experience. Now she sells computers, but previously she worked for a traditional office equipment supplier, who would not train her in new technology. So she bought a computer and enrolled for evening classes. In general, Richmond Survey respondents found it fairly easy to get training which developed their existing job competence, but they had to be more cunning and work harder to acquire new competencies outside the mainstream.

The competency approach helps us shape our future development to suit real needs, but not all competencies contribute equally to high performance. For example, a teacher of junior mathematics must know the subject well enough to deal with all aspects of the syllabus. But additional mathematical knowledge, for example of advanced calculus, isn't needed, and may even be counter-productive. What distinguishes an excellent junior maths teacher from an adequate performer is the capacity to interest, encourage and control children. The careerist should concentrate on acquiring a high standard in those competencies that really matter, i.e. those that relate directly to outstanding performance.

There are no competencies which apply to all jobs; the careerist must identify those that are necessary and, especially, those that result in excellence. It is foolish to rely on conventional wisdom about what distinguishes those who are successful. We should define only relevant skills, knowledge, attitudes and self-concept factors, identifying them by assiduous observation.

Career transitions mean not only that new competencies must be acquired; redundant ones must be dropped. The successful salesman is probably energetic, pushy and outgoing, but sales managers need a different set of competencies in order to perform well; for example, they're likely to be excellent motivators and planners. In fact, some of the competencies which are essential at junior levels are actually unhelpful for more senior roles.

Unlearning is needed. Development requires shedding capability as well as acquiring new competence. Low-level jobs are generally individualistic and results orientated. Senior appointments have much more requirement for team skills, co-operation and decision-making. The careerist with upward ambition must, like a butterfly, go through several stages of metamorphosis.

How can this be managed? Those in the Richmond Survey who rated themselves as 'successfully mobile' gave many illustrations of the personal development techniques they used. The following suggestions were made:

- Identify your next career step specifically
- List people who hold the wanted role at the moment
- Categorize them into 'unsuccessful' and 'successful' performers (be as objective as possible – you don't have to tell them!)
- Get to know both unsuccessful and successful performers personally
- Find out exactly what both low and high performers actually do
- Ask what sort of behaviour contributed to success
- Carefully list the behaviour traits in writing – do not jump to conclusions
- Compare 'best' with 'worst' – what are the differences?
- Go outside your own organization and look at successful performers in the wanted role to validate your conclusions
- Check textbooks, autobiographies and so on to give different perspectives
- Write a detailed description of the competencies needed in the wanted role which result in high performance
- Compare this with your current capabilities and prepare an action plan to fill gaps

The key to competency analysis is detailed exposure to those people who already play the role. Careerists should learn to be analytical without preconceptions. The skills of observation and 'active listening' are needed.

Listening is a competence in itself; it is a technique which is improved by understanding and diligent practice. Those who are rated as good listeners pay attention to others, avoid being distracted and don't confuse data-gathering with making judgements. Most important is the capacity to give relaxed concentration to others for a sustained period of time.

The skilful listener:

- Has 'room' for others (i.e. is not already preoccupied)
- Shows by non-verbal signs that active listening is taking place
- Tells the other person when he or she is ready to listen
- Avoids preconceptions or judgements
- Suppresses the desire to interrupt
- Checks understanding by repeating what is said
- Asks objective, open questions
- Imposes a logical structure to aid understanding
- Respects and values what is being said
- Is prepared to see things from another's point of view

As you listen to high-performing people you will discover what competencies they possess, the perceptions, values, skills, constraints, and feelings which help them perform well. Gradually a picture becomes clearer, like a photographic print developing in a darkroom. The listener must be careful not to be seduced into making judgements or closing down options prematurely.

Long-term career development competencies have to be acquired by individual initiative. The system does not supply careers on a plate. Most organizational training programmes are concerned with developing short-term competencies and are biased towards meeting organizational, not personal, goals. Careerists often gain from experience in several different organizations, but very few companies accept even the principle, let alone facilitate inter-company job changes. However, the training and education industry has improved significantly in the last decade and now provides useful resources for self-development programmes. Things are improving; new media for development are becoming available to assist learning. Careerists ignore education and training opportunities at their peril.

Fortunately, those responsible for training are generally keen to help. They recognize the fact that their role within an organization is somewhat marginal, and they'll often respond to initiatives with enthusiasm. Personal development is usually regarded as a good thing, especially by those at the top. Many careerists have been pleasantly surprised by the responsiveness of organizations. Simon, for example, said: 'I've always found that the Personnel Department are ready to help. Although they're a bit stereotyped, they've provided a lot of practical suggestions. There is nothing a personnel manager enjoys more than being helpful.'

Several of the Richmond Survey respondents felt that the most significant influence on their development came through 'mentors'. Frank is a highly specialized electronics engineer. Aged twenty-nine, he has a curly ginger beard and looks casual even in the best suits. Frank's father was a professor of chemistry, and Frank commented: 'It was taken for granted that I'd do science A-levels and then go to university. It happened quite naturally that I took a degree in physics. Then it seemed obvious that I should do a PhD and become a university lecturer. My first really autonomous choice was to move into a commercial company as a researcher. After I had done this for three or four years I began to want a career in management. The question was, how can a scientist learn about managing? I liked my colleagues and, quite frankly, found great difficulty in thinking like a manager. I can find answers to questions, but I'm not so good at asking them. Although I had a superficial interest in business, I'd never really thought about profit. For me, changing direction into management was the most significant career decision I had ever taken.'

Frank faced a real dilemma: his prestige, relationships and patterns of thought were those of a scientist; management requires very different competencies. He had to acquire the ability to make decisions in confusing situations, use power and influence to get things done, and think like a businessman. Frank needed to place himself in situations in which he would be forced to develop competencies that he lacked. This approach to development is 'action learning', and works on the principle that people learn best by doing, not by comtemplating. In addition, Frank found a 'mentor', who was a guide, supporter, counsellor, disciplinarian and patron. The mentor knew what competencies were needed and created opportunities to enable him to acquire them.

Almost everyone developing a career yearns for a mentor, the occupational equivalent of a wise uncle. During your career, several people will become your mentors. The trick is to find the best person to help you now. A close relationship develops; mentors must get to know you as an individual. Frank illustrated this by reporting that 'my mentor became almost a member of my family'.

Mentoring itself requires special competencies to help people face reality and know their weaknesses, non-strengths and strengths. The mentor should become an expert in giving feedback which is realistic, evaluative and positive. He or she helps the individual perceive and conceptualize in new ways, and assists in reorganizing experiences and identifying key points. Under mentoring and action learning, new competencies are acquired, including informal and political ones.

Frank described the value of his mentor this way: 'I was helped to understand who would support me, who would stab me in the back and how to approach key people. I realized that making progress was partly being right, but largely looking right. My mentor helped me become "streetwise". For example, he told me that the chairman had an irrational but total hatred of men who wore brown shoes, bow ties or beards. Simply dressing correctly was a small step in making good things happen. My mentor had been down the road before me. His experience had come from the university of hard knocks.'

Some organizations have established formal schemes to encourage the mentoring concept. One American company does this by appointing vice-presidents as sponsors of promising young managers in foreign subsidiaries. The mentors take a personal interest in progress, give guidance on careers and informally 'oil the wheels' politically. The scheme is a success because it provides a formal system (based on merit) for introducing promising young men and women to the informal system (based on politics). Most large organizations have some kind of career development system. Careerists should take full advantage of whatever is on offer.

Mentors must be carefully selected. They must have competencies relevant to high performance today. Experience gained in one era may give poor guidelines for the next. Many have been led astray by guidance which merely repeats the past. The mentoring relationship is a learning experience for both. Tony, a company chairman, reported: 'The mentor gains as much as, or more than, the pupil. Making the gift of experience and guidance is meaningful and invigorating. I believe that the mentor role is one of my most important contributions.'

Careerists are well advised actively to seek the highest quality of mentor. This requires:

- Identifying those who can help
- Making overtures and building a constructively dependent relationship
- Developing a 'contract' which informally clarifies what is wanted
- Learning together how to make the relationship work for both

Although a primary function of a mentor is to help the individual gain necessary competencies there is another important role: giving support. Without a support system it's difficult to endure the inevitable strains and uncertainties of an expanding career. The following difficulties are often encountered:

- Declining initiative
- Lapsed motivation
- Low morale
- A sense of isolation
- Uncertainty about personal worth

- Confused personal priorities
- Uncertain values about work and life
- Personal stress

Such career problems are not helped by the external environment. The late twentieth century is cursed with unemployment. The causes are varied but the phenomenon has a vital outcome for those people who are seeking a career: they have to be more flexible, more proactive and more competitive than in a time of full employment. When everyone has a job there is no special requirement to be outstanding. Boom times facilitate career development. When society does not provide opportunities, we have to create them for ourselves. This is a return to the law of the jungle. The Darwinian principle of 'survival of the fittest' is more real to the majority of the population than it has been for many decades. There is little room for the optimistic hope that a cosier employment situation will quickly arise. Self-development is a person's best way to acquire the competencies with which to attack an unfriendly system.

The careerist can't depend on employers to provide all necessary growth experiences. Self-motivated careerists must undertake personal development with or without formal support. This may seem anarchic or revolutionary, but it's not so; organizations and individuals benefit in the end. People must realize that organizations cannot exploit everyone's potential. If the inherent abilities of individuals were fully harnessed, the organization would be swamped with talent and could not cope. In practice, organizations hardly ever have adequate systems for people development. Only the armed services in wartime are an exception. Competition is the rule, and this is probably best for all concerned. It is questionable whether a totally structured career development system is desirable, since it would preclude self-responsibility. While organizations usually provide opportunities for development, it is up to the individuals to capture them. People who sensibly nourish their personal growth are far more likely to survive and succeed.

Competencies alone may not be enough for career management. 'Being' is important. This means enhancing maturity, depth, inner resourcefulness and stature. A career is a great opportunity to deepen yourself. The path we tread in the world, despite all vicissitudes, is a statement of who we are and what we believe to be important. It isn't surprising that some religious traditions see a direct connection between spiritual and worldly development. Hermann Hesse's book *Siddhartha* describes how mystical insights learned in the wilderness during a spiritual quest later enabled the hero to achieve great worldly success.

If depth of character is related to achievement, then logic tells us that career development is incomplete without an element of personal search. From a careful study of career biographies I came to believe that those who achieve high office are clear about their beliefs and values; on the whole they have well-developed personal attributes which provide firm ground on which to build a sound career. Self-knowledge makes a significant contribution to personal energy.

Personal growth comes from the individual, not from the environment. It requires a degree of autonomy discouraged by education systems. Alan explained the ingredients of his own career success and suggested the following guidelines:

- Be conscious of what you are frightened of
- Be prepared to be bold and forceful
- Get broad experience which builds your confidence
- Make contact with seniors (even outside work)
- Take on tasks and achieve visible results
- Become a source of information
- Look good in physical appearance
- Ask yourself: 'How do I present myself non-verbally?'
- Present yourself positively
- Show vigour and energy
- Develop assertive skills
- Avoid self-deprecation
- Avoid being distant from others
- Make yourself the logical choice for the next job

Alan was describing an active stance to self-management. This provides the thrust to identify and acquire the competencies to perform well in each job along the way. Alan, like the other high-achieving careerists in the Richmond Study, demonstrated that an evolving career requires continuing personal growth.

Now complete the project for this section as described. Read this chapter again when you have finished the assignment. This will help to consolidate your learning.

COMPETENCY DEVELOPMENT

For this project you will have to do some research. The purpose is to acquire a personal development plan which will help you achieve your career objectives.

1. Look back to your Step Nine project and read your answer to item 4 (page 223) and list your career objectives for the next year:

   (a)

   (b)

   (c)

   (d)

2. Who are excellent performers of the roles or tasks which you have just listed? (Name people)

   Name one:

   Name two:

   Name three:

Name four:

Name five:

3. Go and talk to as many of these people as possible and ask them:

    (a) What skills they possess
    (b) What knowledge is required
    (c) What attitudes they find constructive
    (d) How they think about their job
    (e) What they have to do well
    (f) What advice they would give to someone new

4. When you have had these conversations (and not before!) use the knowledge and insight you have gained to answer the items below. To meet my career objectives I should:

    (a) Acquire these new competencies:

        (a)

        (b)

        (c)

        (d)

        (e)

    (b) Shed these competencies:

        (a)

(b)

(c)

(d)

(e)

(c) This means I will need to change my behaviour in these ways:

(a)

(b)

(c)

(d)

(e)

(d) I may be able to get help from the following (list people, mentors, training, education etc.):

(a)

(b)

(c)

(d)

(e)

This concludes the project for Step Ten. Don't forget to re-read the chapter before you move to Step Eleven.

STEP ELEVEN

How Can I Make My Own Luck?

'There is a tide in the affairs of men,
Which, taken at the flood, leads on to fortune.'
Shakespeare

CAREER MOVES

For many people the word 'career' is synonymous with moving. The notion was well expressed by Frank, who said, 'I want my career to evolve. For me progress means a series of jobs, each being a step up in terms of status, responsibility and seniority. I want to reach my ceiling.'

Depite the onwards and upwards connotation of the word, some careers do not evolve like released hydrogen-filled balloons. The Richmond Survey included people who had moved in other ways. In fact, careerists have six possible directions for manoeuvre:

- Moving IN (getting a job)
- Moving UP (promotion)
- Moving SIDEWAYS (lateral job change)
- Moving OUT (leaving)
- Moving NOWHERE (consolidating)
- Moving DOWN (setback)

This chapter is concerned with these six basic career manoeuvres. Each is a response to certain needs, requires skilled tactics and carries specific risks. Before we examine them it is useful to ask, 'Why move?'

Career moves are needed to gratify career drivers and to exploit talents. Moves are usually essential. Few people could walk into a job that fulfils and satisfies all personal requirements. Both personal ambition and changes in the world of work require people to make career moves.

There is another important reason for moving. We observed before that most jobs are degenerative on the incumbents. The excitement, stimulation and development inherent in early days are eroded as the job becomes familiar. New challenge is the only proven antidote when a job has exhausted its gifts and becomes tedious and repetitious. Fortunately, a few jobs actually grow with the individual, perhaps those which are entrepreneurial or creative. However, as we discussed in Step Seven, organizations tend to exploit individuals to suit the superior needs of the system, so careerists must expect to outgrow their jobs.

Reasons for career moves are many and varied. All too often these days people experience compulsory change: what George called 'an unexpected job change situation', by which he meant that he was made redundant. Moving has risks and uncertainties, especially as most job-changing takes place in a largely unregularized and opportunistic setting.

MOVING IN

Some careerists demonstrate more moving skills than others. For example, Petra was a personnel officer for an engineering company that halved its workforce in 1981. She coped with the personnel traumas and then was made redundant herself. Her interview is worth quoting at some length as it identifies some of the procedures and skills required to move into another company:

Interviewer: When you learned that you were about to be made redundant what did you do?

Petra: I grieved. The emotions were varied and powerful. For a few days I was in shock. I allowed myself to express how I felt. Then I started to plan.

Interviewer: You began to plan?

Petra: Yes. I decided to search for a job. I carefully analysed my strengths and defined the kind of job I wanted. Then I listed 120 companies in my locality who might need a personnel officer and discovered the names of the personnel directors. There are ways and means of doing this. I wrote to each personnel director by name, tailoring my letter to the particular company. I worked from nine to five on searching.

Interviewer: You got a job by doing this?

Petra: I got three!

Interviewer: Exactly how did it happen?

Petra: One of my letters went to the personnel director of Vast Plc who happened to meet a colleague on a London Underground station. They spoke about my letter. A possible vacancy was available and two weeks later I started.

Interviewer: Did you use any established format for getting a new job?

Petra: No. I thought it up myself. I found opportunities that were just glints in someone's eye. None of the three jobs offered to me had been advertised. But they were there, like pheasants in a wood.

In fact, Petra's series of stratagems were a systematic 'job search'. She undertook a painstaking assessment of herself and the job market, then employed both marketing techniques and guile to flush out and seize opportunities. Petra demonstrated that moving jobs was a task which could be radically improved through the use of good management techniques.

Moving from one organization to another requires effective action planning. Perhaps the best tool is 'force field analysis'. This was developed by Kurt Lewin who saw that all complex situations contain both driving and resisting forces which balance each other; the current situation is an equilibrium between driving and resisting forces.

An example illustrates the concept. Betty was being interviewed for a job. She said, 'I am qualified, eager, available, ready to learn and like the prospective company, but the job is far from home, not well enough paid, and could be temporary.' Using the force field analysis approach we charted the forces like this:

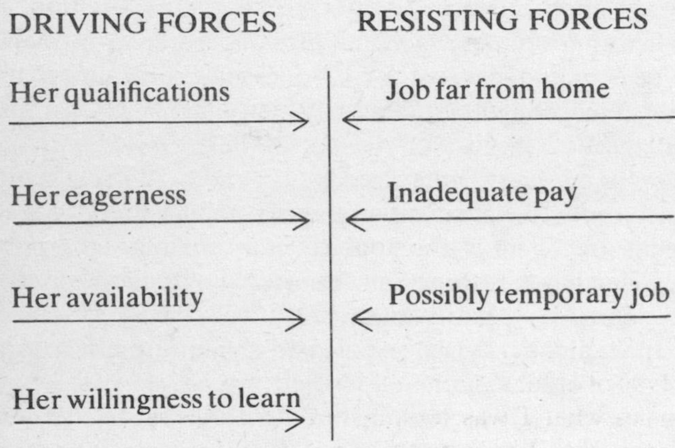

When Betty looked at the chart she spontaneously said, 'Well, the driving forces look right but I must do something to reduce the resisting forces.' This provided her with an action plan. In the end, assurances from the company about pay, a promise of permanent employment and the purchase of a car removed the restraining forces. Betty knew all the factors before she started yet the way the information was displayed was a mini-revelation.

Change is promoted by these three actions:

- Strengthening existing driving forces
- Adding new driving forces
- Reducing or eliminating resisting forces

But, as Lewin observed, the most effective step – reducing the resisting forces – is often considered last. As any judo player knows, the best throws are accomplished by letting positive forces act, rather than trying to push harder.

The careerist intent on moving jobs knows that opportunities are unfairly spread and fortune is partly governed by illogical and obscure principles. Some enjoy many more advantages than others. The best way to manage in an unfair world is to place yourself in areas of high opportunity and then try to exploit the situation.

Consider an example. David, the redundant draughtsman, will shortly be trying to 'move in'. He is now re-training to use computer-aided design equipment. When David's course finishes what will he do? He is well on the way to moving into a new organization, and said, 'I decided to undertake a market analysis exercise. I know that it sounds like jargon but I think that it will really help me. This is the tool to help me plan. I know my objectives and have written a full description of the job I would like to have. Possible job titlcs, the responsibilities I want, what benefits, pay, and perks, the social environment I'd like to work in and the type of organization that I would enjoy.

'Knowing what I was looking for helped, and I have already begun my search. I have considered which organizations offer the opportunities I seek. There are endless sources of information, including recruitment advertisements, journals in my field, reference books in the libraries. Some head-hunters have proved worthwhile. They have their finger on the pulse, as have recruitment agencies. In my polytechnic there are useful career advisers, and, believe it or not, the government agencies are really quite good. Perhaps the most important source of information is personal contacts. My professional society has also proved useful.

'I got the names and addresses of hundreds of possible employers. There is just so much data available. I put it all on my personal computer, like a professional market survey. I talked things over with my wife and we know the geographical areas where we would like to live. Then I made a list of the most promising ten organizations to study in depth. I looked at each as a business analyst, collecting facts about the structure, organization, products or services, reputation, growth pattern, company policy towards people, and their recruitment policy. In fact, I opened a file for each of the ten most promising organizations and asked, "What could I offer this particular organization that would be of value to them?"

'By then I knew a lot. I approached the ten best, through a personal contact if possible. I wrote letters to specific individuals and gave a great deal of thought to presenting myself well. Initially I asked to have the opportunity of talking informally with their design manager as I didn't want my letter to be filed in the wastepaper bin.

'Seven of my target organizations replied, and I had five meetings. Two are about to offer me a job, and one more is dithering.'

David used similar methods to those employed by Petra. They both demonstrated that practical systematic job research makes job-changing a managed and rational process rather than, as one careerist put it, 'blundering through a maze blindfolded with a drunken sot as a guide'.

Organizations employ people to get things done, not to provide work for careerists. With current technology and competitive pressures, organizations have little room for average performers. The need to be marketable was obliquely illustrated by one respondent who told me what he did as a new buyer. He said, 'I decided to attend some sales courses. I wanted to see how the enemy thinks.' Careerists must do the same. They are well advised to put themselves in the mind of an employer, and think about the other's needs. Consider those people you hire to do work for you – even the man who comes to fix the telephone. What do you want employees to do? Typically, the list will include a positive attitude, willingness to work, acceptance of responsibility, and a brisk and effective style. These are general qualities which appeal to customers and bosses alike.

In conclusion, the careerist intent on 'moving in' cannot afford to forget that organizations do not make decisions – people do. A small minority of powerful individuals act as guardians for the organization, and these are the people you have to influence.

MOVING UP

This is the bit you've been waiting for! The most difficult and critical move you will probably undertake is progressing from your present job to a more senior position.

Moving up is the result of many actions, primarily taking initiatives, acquiring necessary competencies and being in the right place at the right time. Baden, now managing director of a service company, gave a number of valuable insights into promotion in his interview. He said, 'People have to realize that pyramids have little room at the apex and so only the exceptional get there. Like making money on the Stock Exchange, if it was easy everyone would do it. Here are some guidelines.

'Get a track record for success by assuming responsibilities and getting things done, and looking good. Be associated with success and avoid being associated with failure. Also find out how the jobs above you are actually acquired and mould yourself to fit the requirements, whilst not prejudicing your dignity. Find problems which are hurting someone powerful and contribute to solving them. Easing someone else's pain is a potent thing to do. Don't be too rigid; remember the strongest tree bends with the prevailing wind yet retains its integrity. Develop a different approach to each organization you work in. Always take great care to tune yourself to suit your prospective host. Try not to be negative, even when you feel critical. Bosses don't like to have a burr under their saddle.

'Also, I think it is important to make it clear that you are prepared to move. Exploit personnel resources – they may not help but they ought to be in contact with those who can. Get on the database which most organizations keep, listing their promising people. This means taking active steps to get out from under bosses who try to keep you down.

'Make it possible for you to be replaced by developing your successors, but be careful of making yourself totally redundant! Timing is of the essence. Make yourself indispensable when you are establishing your track record and then be free to take advantage of the kudos success brings.'

When moving up you are vulnerable. Possibly people will attempt to take advantage of you. One practical piece of advice is to try to negotiate a good contract when you enter. A good contract will spell out your role and what is expected of you. This was well expressed by Norma, the film editor. She said, 'I am a freelance film editor which means that I work by the day, month or year to someone who wants film cut. I've learned that whenever I take a new assignment it pays to be clear about the facilities I need, my standards of work, and my status in the production team. I will not sit there and be directed by a spotty Oxford graduate on his fifth week of training even if he thinks that he is the incarnation of David Lean. I know what I need to do a good job. I make sure, in the nicest possible way, that everyone knows where I stand.' Knowing where you stand and what is expected of you is very important to careerists and is considered in greater detail in Step Twelve.

A most important question that the upwardly mobile careerist must face is how to 'travel'. Some decide to follow well-trodden paths, others venture into the undergrowth where few have walked before, and many will take the river – bobbing along like a cork driven by the current. Each means of travel can be progressive but is based on a different view of how the world operates.

Conservatives prefer established routes and see the world as an organized place; radicals see the world as volatile and evolving where adventurers win; the happy-go-lucky prefer easy routes and see the world as benign and bountiful.

Conservatives, radicals and happy-go-lucky careerists can all find evidence to support their stances. Certainly, all three attitudes seem to be effective in certain situations. Conservatives build solid careers in predictable bureaucracies, radicals thrive in market-orientated smaller organizations, whilst the happy-go-lucky gather opportunities as they occur.

Those in the Richmond Survey who had moved up more than three levels in the past five years were asked about the role of personal contacts in facilitating their advance. The consensus of opinion was that personal relationships are always important but conscious exploitation of others was potentially counter-productive. Those with power are alert to being used to fulfil the self-aggrandizing aims of others. Understandably, they deprecate manipulation, however subtle it is. Anyone who seeks to exploit friendship is likely to find that personal relationships are harmed and no advantage is gained.

This is contrary to advice given by some career specialists who exhort careerists to exploit personal contacts as many opportunities arise through patronage or 'the old boys network'. These specialists advise careerists to gather contacts like a schoolboy collects postage stamps, and then exploit them for information, largesse and 'connection power'.

It is certainly true that contacts can be a vehicle for career progress, but this works best when the help comes freely from the senior. This is most likely to be gained by careerists who are reluctant to exploit unfair advantage.

As one survey member, Bob, said, 'I have always found that it is better to be bought than sell myself. I believe in doing a good job. People are not fools. They know that they have to look beneath the surface and see how good I really am. I try to be transparent and yet present my achievements favourably. I make a point of being open, outgoing and honest. Being truthful, I'm conscious that by obviously not selling myself I am in fact selling.' Another respondent, Petra, gave a different reason for consciously not manipulating others. She pointed out, 'You might be able to acquire a new responsibility by being cunning but keeping the job is another matter. I've seen too many people be promoted badly, and then get slung out. Much better to be selected on the basis of what you can do. False advertising might sell a product, but the user soon learns that he has bought a dud.'

This 'fair dealing' approach to moving up is based on the principle that honesty and openness pay. The emphasis on 'authenticity' has another advantage which was clearly described by Richard, who commented, 'Deciding to be open, honest and direct helped my self-confidence. I really worked at being myself. Somehow being truthful gave me strength. People commented that I gained in stature.'

It is not surprising that fair dealing is an effective strategy for moving up. One of the principles of successful interpersonal relationships is reciprocity: what is given should balance with what is taken. Careerists want advantage and so must consider what they can give in return. Why should someone devote their efforts to help you?

MOVING SIDEWAYS

Those who wish eventually to rise to positions of power and influence find that most organizations restrict their advance because they fail to give the breadth of experience needed for senior roles. Ironically, the creative and developmental benefits of sideways moves are most clearly seen in the career experiences of the sons and daughters of ruling families. Tony is now in a very senior position. His son, now twenty-two, is about to leave university with a degree in archaeology. Tony spent some time during his interview discussing his son's future career route:

Interviewer: What plans do you have for your son's career?

Tony: He needs some hard knocks. I want to expose him to the gritty world of getting things done. He must come in contact with the working class. It's time he started to learn about the real world.

Interviewer: You will take him into your own organization then?

Tony: Of course, but I'll put him with someone very good who will both expose him to the harsh realities but not let him get swamped.

Interviewer: What is his likely career progress?

Tony: Perhaps eighteen months as a trainee industrial engineer, a period as a supervisor, then out on the road selling. Perhaps a couple of big projects, then a Masters degree in business from Harvard, Stanford or McGill. After this he should work in Finance and Marketing before doing a mini-managing director's job somewhere. Then we'll see how good he is.

Interviewer: A broad base of functional training.
Tony: Yes. Top management needs depth and breadth. At each stage he'll work with the best people, but will have to perform.
Interviewer: Would you give this breadth of training to anyone else?
Tony: If they showed great talent, then we would.
Interviewer: How would you recognize such talent?
Tony: The cream must rise to the top of the milk.

This interview was most informative. It demonstrated that Tony knew that sideways moves are essential preparation for senior roles. No doubt there were dozens of young men and women in Tony's organization with the same potential as his son. They needed a breadth of experience but would not get it unless they took the initiative for themselves.

Careerists who wish to move up organizations find they have to move sideways several times in order to broaden their experience to handle senior jobs. For example, a managing director must be able to direct and integrate the efforts of marketing, finance, production, sales, personnel, research and planning functions. Without such expertise the managing director is vulnerable, as George's experience showed. He said, 'I was an accountant who had made good. They were looking for an MD and I volunteered. It was a case of too much to learn too quick. Marketing were spending money like drunken sailors, manufacturing seemed unable to produce a reliable product and no one talked to R & D who were known as the "funny farm". I saw the problems but couldn't put them right. I didn't know who needed to be stroked, who should have the boot, and which people required their heads banged together. By the time I got the job almost sorted out the boss lost patience and I was out on my ear.'

Breadth of experience is best gained early. By the time someone is over thirty years old they are likely to be too expensive and too valuable at what they are doing to move sideways. Far-sighted organizations take appropriate people out of responsible jobs and place them in learner roles. But careerists cannot depend on organizations: they must be ready to take the initiative themselves.

Of course, not all sideways moves are part of the long-term game of chess that careerists must play. Another reason for sideways moves is that a current specialization is out of phase with the person's drivers or talents.

I have come to believe that it is very important to choose a career line which corresponds with the emotional flow of the individual. Walter, now a personnel director, began his career training to be an accountant. He described the experience graphically: 'As a trainee accountant I felt like a piece of wood being planed against the grain. Each new experience was abrasive and uncomfortable. Then I decided to get into a people-orientated job. It meant a sideways move and a lot of new study. Suddenly I was a piece of wood turned end on and the plane was cutting with the grain. Everything seemed to be in harmony. There was no doubt that this was my thing.'

Moving sideways requires the same management skills as moving up. It rarely happens by chance, especially to mature careerists, and it can be an exciting, invigorating and developmental career step.

MOVING OUT

People move out of organizations for three reasons: to join another organization; to escape; because they are pushed.

We've discussed joining another organization in order to move sideways or upwards; escaping is a different matter. Sometimes organizations are coercive or inhospitable, inhibiting the individual from growing or being themselves. In Step Seven we discussed how organizations offered different career experiences. Someone stuck in an organization which does not suit their drivers or utilize their talents may need to escape.

As prisoners of war testify, escaping is a complex and arduous matter. Tunnels may have to be secretly dug under the watchful eyes of the guards. This point was well made by Jerry who said, 'I was working for ABC retailers as a management trainee and it became apparent to me that I would never fit their mould. ABC programmed their managers to think in narrow channels, and I hated it. I wanted to get out but needed a focus. Eventually I found a small group of professional fund raisers who were looking for a new member. This looked attractive, so, after much heart searching, I left ABC and became an apprentice fund raiser. This suited my wish to be more my own master. Leaving ABC was hard but they don't want semi-rebels. I had to get very clear about what I wanted. Fund raising offered the right blend of autonomy, a chance to learn and a loose kind of organization. It fulfilled me for five years.'

Career escapers have to be especially creative and radical. They feel wrongly positioned yet the inertia of their existing work role takes them down a narrow path towards somewhere they don't want to go. The mould has to be broken. Those visioning techniques we described in Step Eight become vital. Escape without a plan is a dangerous enterprise.

Sometimes people want to escape from dead-end careers. Adrian gave useful information to the Richmond Survey but did not give a complete interview so he is not included in the sample. He is a highly intelligent but prickly twenty-six-year-old disadvantaged by his past. He commented, 'Frankly, I was lazy at school. When I was just sixteen my father lost his temper for the ninth time and said to me, "Either you work hard at school or get a job." I joined the army, staying for five years as signaller. After the army I drifted from job to job, usually leaving after a row with the boss. Along the way I acquired a child, then a wife, and decided it was time to settle down and begin a career, properly. But I can't get started. I have few qualifications and my CV looks appalling. At the moment I am painting white lines on tennis courts. Really, I don't know which way to go.' Adrian is the victim of choices made when he was much younger. This often happens – someone who has served a prison sentence experiences the same problem even more intensively. A gambler would say that the cards were stacked against him. Adrian has four choices:

- Accept his lot and continue to paint lines on tennis courts

How Can I Make My Own Luck?

- Gradually build up a 'better hand' by improving his qualifications
- Find new ways to market himself to potential employers
- Play a 'different game' (change career, location or his expectations)

Should you wish to move out, or are being pushed out, you need *Managing Your Own Career* and all the help you can get. It is a time of turbulence and even traumatic shock. If you haven't already done so you are well advised to work systematically through this book starting at Step One. Also, go to your local library and find out about job search skills. This is a topic in itself and has only been lightly touched in this book. (The best book for you is *What Colour is Your Parachute?* by Richard Bolles, published in the UK by Umbrella Publishing Services Ltd, 9 Fitzroy Square, London W1P 6AE.)

MOVING NOWHERE

Many times we have reiterated that a satisfying career is a good fit between person and his or her work life. The notion of movement is widely associated with the word career but this can become a trap for the unwary. Becoming emotionally identified with progress for its own sake is likely to prove unfulfilling. A few Richmond Survey respondents spoke scathingly of the 'rat race' and its destructive elements. Andrew, now a financial director, discussed this with great feeling:

Interviewer: In your earlier career you had a very intensive job?

Andrew: Yes, I was the financial hit man for an international company. I was living out of a suitcase. The cupboard was stuffed with duty free liquor. I liked the jetset image but it did nothing for my lifestyle.

Interviewer: Tell me about your experience.

Andrew: Frankly, two bad things happened. I took to drink and my wife had a bit of a breakdown. She felt unsettled and all sorts of things started to go wrong.

Interviewer: What lessons did you learn from the experience?

Andrew: I learned that some companies are vampires. They will suck out all of a man's energy, screw up his lifestyle and then ask for more. We're attracted to gaudy baubles like savages. It's pathetic.

Interviewer: You clearly feel bitter.

Andrew: Too right. I was seduced. Of course, I was a willing participant in a way, but they raped me. One year I was away from home for 154 days. My wife couldn't be satisfied with an arrangement like that. We fell apart.

Interviewer: The situation is resolved now?

Andrew: Yes, but after a lot of pain. I had to readjust my priorities. I put my family first now. My career horizons are limited by my lifestyle. It won't happen again. I'm sticking.

Andrew's career history demonstrates the dilemma of success. Upwardly mobile people, especially in early career, tend to give a huge commitment to their jobs. This is expected by bosses watchful for bright talent. Some individuals may choose to move nowhere in order to preserve their quality of life.

The choice not to move is also a necessary strategy for those learning from their jobs. Probably the last thing someone in an intensive growth phase should do is move. New competencies must be consolidated before the person goes on to bigger and better things. Otherwise personal development drags behind capability: a dangerous mismatch. This was described elegantly by Alan who said, 'I have always felt that careers have natural rhythms like skiing. There is a time for taking easy pistes, then something more difficult must be attempted. Good instruction should be followed by a fast downhill run to consolidate the lessons learned. The secret is to push oneself only 10 per cent above the comfort level; otherwise bones get broken and confidence vanishes.'

The final reason for moving nowhere is that doors have been closed. Many people have inertia thrust upon them. Not everyone chooses to stay put. They become stuck. They may feel ready to tackle a bigger or different job but someone, somewhere has decided that job change is not for them. Sometimes such decisions reflect the truth – that the person has risen to 'the level of incompetence'. Then the careerist is well advised to curb his or her ambition and simply do a good job. If, after a thorough and painstaking analysis, the careerist feels unjustly treated, then the remedy is to move out.

MOVING DOWN

Not all careers are upward climbs. Setbacks occur and prove to be a testing time. Most large organizations are unwilling to demote a person as this demonstrates that someone made a mistake in the original appointment. People who are demoted, however, are likely to have significant flaws of competence, and their best initial response is to try to learn from the experience. This was well described by Roger, the civil engineer:

Roger: My career suffered a big setback when I was twenty-seven.
Interviewer: Tell me more.
Roger: Frankly, I was demoted. I'd been given a job in Saudi to build a pumping station and the whole thing was a cock-up from start to finish. You name it, it went wrong. And it was my fault. I set the job up badly, got intimidated by the hairy-kneed site foreman and made some planning mistakes.
Interviewer: It sounds like a bad experience.
Roger: The worst thing was that I built an access road three metres from where it should be. The job was a mess.
Interviewer: What happened?
Roger: They brought me back to the UK, kicked me hard, and then sent me back under an experienced engineer to finish the job. I had to eat humble pie but learnt such a hell of a lot. It took two years before they even began to trust me again.

Interviewer: How do you reflect on this now?
Roger: The best thing, professionally, that ever happened to me!

Roger demonstrated that wise careerists learn from mistakes and setbacks. He was fortunate because his employer gave him the opportunity to put right what had gone wrong. Over a ten-year period he has gained, not suffered, through this experience.

Of course, many demotions have less constructive outcomes, especially for older people. Periodically, a new wave of bright people replace the old guard. Tony, the company chairman, commented on this when he said, 'An organization of any size becomes highly dependent on the quality of its leader. An incompetent individual holding a position of power is a cancer. Around and under him the organization rots. As a chairman I have to ensure that leadership is honourable, visionary, practical and intelligent. If anyone holding power fails to perform, then I'll take action. Phase one is counselling, phase two is training and phase three is "out". The Tsars of Russia were making a managerial bodge and they had to go. Quite right, too.'

Careers can collapse like a house of cards. One afternoon I met a general manager from a weapons research company. He walked out of a supermarket carrying a bottle of whisky which had not been paid for. At the subsequent court appearance a minor fine was imposed. Much more serious was the associated publicity which resulted in his company asking for a letter of resignation. They claimed, with good reason, that no one with a tainted reputation could hold down a high-security job. So the ex-general manager found himself, in his early fifties, looking for a job without any psychological preparation. All his previous thinking had been orientated to a stable corporate career structure. In this case, the story has an unhappy outcome. He failed to find another job which matched his somewhat extravagant expectations and shortly afterwards developed an illness which doctors found difficult to identify. A semi-invalid life ensued. There is one important lesson to be learnt from this story: in every career there are actions or inactions which can have catastrophic effects.

Moving down can be a learning experience, the result of victimization (a sacrificial lamb), or it can be the closing chapter of a career. If, unlike the Phoenix, the person is unable or unwilling to rise from the ashes, then a constructive use of career energy is to turn outside the organization and seek to gratify drivers and express talents elsewhere.

The project for this section requires you to think about the moves you are likely to take in the next year. Keep referring to this chapter to refresh your mind as you complete the exercise. Then proceed to the final step. Keep it up – you're nearly there!

TO MOVE OR NOT TO MOVE?

This project will help you consider whether a career move is desirable and what should happen. Look back to your career objectives on page 222 in Step Nine. Refresh your mind about your decisions. Do they still look right to you? If not, revise the objectives before you proceed.

Answer each item below comprehensively and progress methodically. Spend at least five minutes on each item; superficial analysis is not helpful.

1. What career moves are implicit or explicit in your next year's plan (Step Nine, item 4 on page 223)?

   (a)

   (b)

   (c)

2. Looking at your longer-term vision of the future (Step Eight, item 5 on page 206), what career moves are desirable or necessary in the longer term?

   (a)

   (b)

(c)

(d)

(e)

3. Review your answers to questions 1 and 2 and specify the next most practical and desirable career move you could make (in detail):

4. Do you want to move 'in', 'up', 'sideways', 'out', 'nowhere' or 'down'?

5. Review the relevant section on moving in this chapter. What steps should you take to give you the best chance of moving successfully?

   (a)

   (b)

   (c)

   (d)

   (e)

6. What are the primary difficulties you face in making such a move?

   (a)

   (b)

   (c)

   (d)

   (e)

That completes your work for Step Eleven. Don't move on until you know what your next career moves should be. Maybe other possibilities will emerge, but ensure your plan is crystal clear so you can judge them.

STEP TWELVE

How Can I Best Exploit the Present?

'If not now, when?'
Hillel 'The Elder'

MAKING THE BEST OF THE PRESENT

We've almost reached the end. By now you have taken a good look at yourself and thought deeply about the world of work. You have a vision for the future and a plan. This final step considers how you can exploit your current work role.

Jobs are many and varied. We may work at an antique desk in a huge wood-panelled office, behind the wheel of a bus, or standing with a dentist's drill peering at a decaying molar. Some of you may be reading this book in an unemployment office queue or behind the locked doors of a prison cell. Each occupational role offers some opportunities for achieving satisfaction and learning, and for contributing to others.

I believe that concentration on 'now' is most important. Several respondents in the Richmond Survey alerted me to the hazards of over-emphasizing the future. One of them put it this way: 'Today is the first day of the rest of your career. Each day we should ask how can I get the most out of doing this? That's the way to make progress.'

It was interesting that those respondents who felt satisfied with their current career progress were careful to pay attention to the present. They would reflect for a while on possible visions of the future, then roll up their sleeves and get on with their current work.

Tim plainly expressed the need to master the present before grasping the future when he said, 'I see a lot of bright young things with plenty of ambition but no substance. This isn't the way to build a career. Those who do well are likely to be bloody good at their jobs and take care to learn from experience.'

Tim was one of several who cogently argued that careerists should deliberately exploit every work situation. He gave an interesting example: 'When I was a graduate trainee I was asked to perform a complicated photocopying job. I was standing at the copier feeling a bit pissed off as the job was beneath me. The boss came along and started a conversation. He pointed out that I was not working efficiently and said something I will never forget: "Use every situation to learn how to do something better." In the next hour I tried to become super efficient and learnt a lot. All this from photocopying!'

Learning can be difficult in demanding jobs because so much effort is invested in keeping on top of the work that the person 'becomes the job'. Arthur explained this well: 'As an electronics engineer I devoted every ounce of mental energy to doing my job. I did not give any thought to myself. One day I woke up to find that my career was being left to chance.'

We have already argued that careerists cannot afford to become totally identified with their jobs. They must actively manage their careers, which requires a degree of self-awareness and a strategy for exploiting the present.

When the Richmond Survey interviews were analysed it became clear that there are four strategies for job exploitation:

- Reducing 'negative' elements to an absolute minimum
- Building in as many 'positive' features as possible
- Using today's experience to help you prepare for the future
- Making a useful contribution

We will examine each strategy separately.

REDUCING THE NEGATIVE

Of course careerists should try to reduce negative aspects of their jobs, but this is less simple than it seems. It is necessary carefully to answer the question, 'What is negative?' Take an example: many teenagers don't like washing themselves, disliking water as much as the family cat. Yet being clean is neither meaningless nor unconstructive. Washing, as parents never tire of telling their pungent children, is an essential attribute of a civilized human being. Merely disliking an activity does not make it negative. This is also true in relation to career-building. Bob made the point clearly when he stated: 'I hated the disciplines when I began to study law but I've come to respect my training as excellent and essential preparation for a legal career.' In fact, almost all respondents in the survey reported that they often disliked early disciplines but later regarded them as being extremely useful.

Even very demanding situations are not necessarily negative. Katherine said, 'I went through a nasty stage where I was totally overburdened. Although it was an awful time and fantastically stressful I now feel that it was a major growth experience. I realized that I could not worry about every little thing and had to learn not to go to pieces. I now can cope with everything that is thrown at me.' Katherine had learned to thrive under pressure and found this capability was invaluable. We need to be stretched to find our limits.

Neither dislike nor demand are negative job elements by definition. For careerists, a negative job element is any characteristic which blocks satisfaction of career drivers or expression of talents. Jobs only become manacles when they aren't profitable or fun or developmental.

Almost every job has negative elements. Paraphrasing Professor Pugh of the Open University, 'Any job has the weaknesses of its strengths.' In other words, all occupations result in uneven development. Boxers are not noted for their intellectual capabilities; priests are not highly regarded as fighters. Through exploiting one talent you neglect another; specialization has costs as well as benefits.

Organizations encourage specialization. Division of labour is the guideline of industrial society. Corporations break down work into discrete packages to develop expertise. They come to depend on people with essential specialized competencies. Personnel experts identify such key people and try to 'nail their feet to the ground'. It may suit the careerist in the short term to be cosseted in this way by a benign and appreciative organization, but the longer-term career advantages of providing a narrow specialized service are more suspect. Today's key workers can become tomorrow's obsolete human resources. It is an asset to acquire those specializations which have long-term marketable advantages.

Careerists can rarely escape periods of frustration and excessive specialization. This is what organizations are prepared to pay for, and there is little real choice. Endurance is a necessary attribute. Alan put it this way: 'At some stage, perhaps for long stretches of time, the role you occupy may be far from satisfactory. Aspects will infuriate you, dull your senses or feel like a sentence on a treadwheel.' Several respondents commented that negative job elements must not become sources of irritation or bitterness. Avoiding such negative reactions keeps up morale and maintains a good public image. As a personnel director, Walter understood this clearly: 'Those who have power to decide the fate of others are looking for good performers. They are suspicious of those who are full of woe. I advise everyone to make the best of their current job, and clearly to demonstrate high performance. This does not imply that people should just accept their lot. In general, people do not make enough fuss if they are stuck. They should make a noise saying "recognize me". Not a little noise, as the system will drown that out. A big, but decent, noise.'

Negative experiences in a job can lead to a regressive cycle. Zia, whose frantic job history was briefly described earlier, admitted, 'I used to get myself in a frame of mind where the whole job felt like purgatory. I didn't try to perform well. The boss saw me slacking and would try to sort me out. I reacted badly. The whole thing used to go from bad to worse.'

The message was summarized by James who said, 'I've been in

many bad job situations. It is almost inevitable that one will be in the doldrums for part of the time. At first, I found this depressing and frustrating. Now, I concentrate on exploiting what I've got. This helps me and helps the boss. Nothing gets up people's noses more than someone who is a world expert at being a pain in the arse.'

Richmond Survey respondents found it helpful to specify negative job elements. There was much useful learning to be gained by overcoming obstacles. Common issues were:

- Feeling stuck (typical remedy: rework aims and objectives, then move)
- Apparently closed doors (typical remedy: develop new competencies)
- Feeling undervalued (typical remedy: clearly demonstrate talents)
- Having stopped growing (typical remedy: move)
- Feeling overstretched (typical remedy: restructure current work load)
- Uncongenial supervision/co-workers (typical remedy: take a firm stand)

Some job characteristics are defined as negative even though they contribute to the individual's career progress. The explanation is that they undermine the quality of life. The Richmond Study illustrated that working and private lives are intimately connected, especially for those with 'middle-class' careers. The interrelationship has also been described by other researchers. *Must Success Cost So Much?* (Grant McIntyre, London 1980), a study by Paul Evans and Fernando Bartolome conducted at INSEAD, the European School of Business Administration, examined the career histories of 532 men, all 'successful' middle managers. Three phases were clearly distinguishable. The first phase up to about the age of thirty-five is concerned with launching a career. In the second phase, lasting perhaps a decade, most managers concentrated more on their private lives. Some of the probable neglect of the first phase was redressed. The third identifiable phase, lasting until the mid-fifties, integrates life and work. Both the Richmond and INSEAD studies conclude that with careful management professional and private lives can complement and enhance each other. The commonly accepted stereotype that success comes to workaholics, exploiters, and potential heart attack victims is false. With intelligent self-interest a successful career need not destroy the quality of private life.

BUILDING IN POSITIVE ELEMENTS

Those who rated themselves good at exploiting their current jobs emphasized that it is vital to take a 'helicopter' viewpoint – rise above immediate concerns and place experiences in context. Such people adopt the attitude that today's experience should make a useful contribution to long-term aims and objectives.

A developmental job may arise by accident, but the careerist cannot rely on such serendipity. Fortunately, it is often possible to take initiatives which change the structure of a job. Assertion is the relevant competence. This requires clearly putting points in ways which increase the possibility of effective influence. Through assertion the careerist takes action to try to build positive elements into the job.

Whilst talking about building a positive job, Walter used the phrase 'psychological contract'. This proved to be a most useful concept. A psychological contract is an explicit agreement between two involved parties about who is going to do what for whom by when. The contract may or may not be written down, but it covers all the important aspects of the relationship. Walter described a psychological contract clearly when he said, 'I have found that it is vital to know exactly what is expected of me. I ask these eight questions whenever I am uncertain about a job and I record the answers:

- Why does this job exist?
- What are the objectives?
- Which are the most important objectives?
- How will I know when I am successful?
- Which other individuals/departments should I develop a good relationship with?
- What discretion do I have to spend money and other resources?
- What style of leadership should I use?
- Where should I turn for help if I have a problem?

'I have learned, through bitter experience, that each question must be answered in depth. I take the attitude that I must get everything 100 per cent clear or I will be screwed. It takes hours to sort this out but, believe me, it pays. When agreement has been reached I give the boss an impeccably typed summary and then get on.'

Although Walter chose to formalize a psychological contract, he went on to emphasize that it was important to avoid being excessively rigid. He knew that verbal agreements must be reinforced by behaviour if they are to be real, and contracts need to be updated as things change. Insistence on legalistic procedures is seen as unconstructive rigidity. Another respondent, Tony, spoke scathingly of a member of his staff who attempted to agree a contract by manipulation. He commented, 'My commercial director was under pressure. He came in one morning wanting to review his objectives. From the way he spoke I knew that he'd read some self-help management book and was trying out a new technique on me. I played along for a while but saw red when he tried to lumber all his responsibilities on to everyone else.' Sustainable psychological contracts are fair and protective for both sides. They provide a mechanism to build positive elements into jobs.

Jobs exist in a human environment. People make a difference, especially the boss. A fair and friendly boss can make a dull job bearable whereas an unfair, miserable, exploitative or incompetent boss is able to taint every work experience without trying. Building a constructive relationship with the boss is an essential prelude to negotiating a positive job.

PREPARING FOR THE FUTURE

Simply doing a good job and waiting to be recognized is a risky career strategy. A non-assertive stance is encouraged in schools, where self-promotion is maligned. But high achievement at work often goes unrecognized unless the careerist achieves visibility. Gilbert and Sullivan expressed the point beautifully in the line: 'Blow your own trumpet or, trust me, you haven't a chance.'

The competence to sell oneself is high in those whose careers are moving. As we noted earlier, self-marketing is a two-edged sword. Like the perfect omelette it should be neither under- nor overdone. The underselling careerist is readily passed over, whereas the overselling careerist is perceived as a windbag and a fool.

A careful study of the selling techniques of Richmond careerists revealed that several methods had proved effective. These were:

- Being pro-establishment – adopting the basic values of the bosses
- Being helpful – working to be obviously constructive in all situations
- Distinction – finding ways to stand out from the crowd
- Communicating achievements – letting others appreciate your success
- Building trust – demonstrating reliability
- Building stature – acquiring the ability to rise above immediate issues and concerns and place experience in context
- Gaining visibility – becoming known to those with power
- Articulating a vision – being seen as someone who can create or improve the future
- Showing pragmatism – being able to get things done

It's today's tasks which give the opportunity to sell yourself. Everything counts all the time. Even subtleties of non-verbal presentation, like physical stance, voice timbre and eye contact matter. But it is inadvisable to mould oneself into an ideal. As Caroline said, 'The essence of self-promotion is to have the confidence to be oneself, but to be always conscious of which parts to allow expression.'

Those careerists who sustain demanding jobs talk about the importance of personal presentation. Katherine put this especially clearly when she said, 'People do not remember you for the twenty things you do well, but for the one thing you do badly. It's important to be both successful and to be seen as successful. Even shy and reticent people have to learn to blow their trumpets.'

One way of self-promotion was greatly favoured: undertaking projects which have a tangible output. Merely 'doing a good job' gives insufficient visibility for the careerist. Tasks which have clearly indentifiable end products are great opportunities. Despite the risk of public failure, the careerist is well advised to undertake assignments which have obvious results. One respondent emphasized this by saying, 'I've learned that it is important to be seen as the owner of good things. I can make an impression in half a day that will benefit me for years.'

The good salesman begins by believing in the product. For the careerist, 'the product' is a combination of work history and presentation today. As people are judged on the basis of their track record they must shine in whatever job they happen to hold at the present time.

The term 'track record' comes from horse racing. I first learned about this from my father who introduced me to the mysteries of gambling when I was about twelve. He loved racing and, not surprisingly, enjoyed backing winners. My father was a rare gambler; he actually made a profit from his pastime. I would watch him studying the weekly 'form book'. Bets were made only after considerable thought. I remember him advising me that 'Gamblers minimize risk. They depend on history. There are six aspects of a track record – breeding, training, form, handicap, jockey and going. All of these need to be weighed up.' My father pointed out that 'It is the bookmakers who have the big cars and fat cigars. The odds are stacked in their favour. If you want to win, then you have to become smarter than Mr Average. The secret is study track records.'

For the careerist a good track record is all-important. Despite many years of studying psychology I have not found a better way of assessing track records than my father's 'breeding, training, form, handicap, jockey and going' approach. After all, he did beat the bookmakers at their own game!

First we will define the words in terms which make sense to careerists:

'Breeding' – inherited capability
'Training' – the extent to which latent capability has been developed
'Form' – readiness to perform to the best standard
'Handicap' – the extent to which constraints limit performance
'Jockey' – the quality of the supervisor
'Going' – whether the immediate environment helps or hinders

Acquiring a marketable track record requires diligence over years, perhaps decades. It is helpful to think about yourself from the perspective of a professional gambler. What is your breeding, training, form, handicap, jockey and going? Weigh up the odds and be wary of investing in outside chances. Keep asking, 'How can I profitably exploit this opportunity?' Try to avoid excessive optimism (like my butcher who thinks he can run the country better than the Prime Minister) or unwarranted pessimism (feeling that any change is likely to end up for the worse).

Roger made a very interesting point in his interview. He had observed that what the careerist did not do was as important as what was actually done. The interview is worth quoting at some length:

Interviewer: What steps do you take to make the most of your current job?

Roger: Well, I do all the good things but, most important, I've learnt when to say 'no'. For instance, I won't allow myself to become bogged down with trivia, or get into side waters. I do not undertake excessively gruelling tasks except in an extreme emergency. I take painstaking steps to avoid having to meet unrealistic deadlines or expectations.

Interviewer: You feel that you have to take a firm stand.

Roger: That's right. I will not become someone's cat's-paw. No one takes you seriously unless you are a person to be reckoned with. Fame and fortune never went to a pipsqueak.

Interviewer: How can this be done?

Roger: It's a question of building a reputation. If people know that you contribute then they will accept that you won't be kicked around.

MAKING A CONTRIBUTION

In a book of this sort it is tempting to concentrate exclusively on helping individuals exploit the world around them. Whilst this has merit, and is an accurate reflection of the way people may think, there is another side to be considered. Careerists told me that it is important to ask, 'What am I contributing to the community?'

Most careers are forged in a competitive environment. Indeed, competition is part of many people's definition of a 'good career'. Some people succeed, some partly succeed and others fail! Careering, for most of the Richmond Survey respondents, was about succeeding. This meant that careerists had to learn to fight and win. One respondent, Andrew, stated, 'I have always been prepared to fight but I try to do it ethically. There are certain rules to follow.' The criteria for 'fair fighting' are helpful. They are:

- Use merit and arguments
- Avoid intimidation or game-playing
- Explicitly state what you want
- Don't punish losers

- Redouble your efforts when you are disadvantaged
- Try to win for the other person too if at all possible

These criteria were considered important for four reasons.

First, over-emphasizing what you want encourages blind selfishness and reduces sensitivity to the market.

Secondly, the acquisition of advantage (the goal of many careerists) places a moral burden on the privileged to discharge their responsibilities with care and consideration.

Thirdly, it has long been recognized that giving to others encourages and strengthens the giver. People gain through making a contribution to the world about them.

Fourthly, if everyone pursued self-advantage to the exclusion of other motives, then the quality of society would degenerate to such an extent that no one would enjoy a fulfilling career.

Three comments by respondents who had risen much higher than others alerted me to this point. Each was asked, 'What is the purpose of your career?' They replied:

'My career is my way of giving back some of the benefits I have been given.'

'I want to make an impact by being a net contributor to the world. For me the notion of service is not dead.'

'I work primarily to satisfy myself. This requires that I believe that what I do has some real worth. A working lifetime is too long to be frittered away on trivia.'

Close acquaintance with those who achieve high office has made me less cynical about the effects of power. In the main I have been impressed with the people who rise to the top. They think widely and care about their responsibilities. Some have acquired a great depth of insight and wisdom. Of course, power has been gained by exploiters and fools, but in general the credentials of those who 'rise to the top of the milk' are impressive.

There is a British tradition that power and service should go hand in hand. From the notion that success brings both rights and duties it follows that career growth requires moral development. For example, a hospital cleaner is responsible for sweeping corridors but the head of a teaching hospital makes decisions which affect the health care of tens of thousands of people. As responsibility increases, so does the need to be right.

All societies are hierarchical with power being unevenly distributed. Those who reach top positions become guardians of the community. When a person's career is directed upwards he or she must come to a point where they ask, 'What am I contributing to the world around me?' If the answer is 'nothing', then I believe little real satisfaction will be gained. After all, your career is probably the largest contribution you will make to the community at large.

IN CONCLUSION

A 'career' can mean many things. It may prove venturesome or dull, stretching or confining, fruitful or fruitless. Those of us who live in the Western world have an opportunity unimagined by our forefathers: we have more freedom to sculpt our careers than was ever dreamt possible. I trust the career you begin today is good for you.

There is one last project to undertake. Don't flag now! Get the job done, and good fortune.

EXPLOIT YOUR JOB

This project encourages you to think about your present job critically. Spend about an hour on it and then complete the final assignment.

1. My current job title is:

2. My main responsibilities are:

   (a)

   (b)

   (c)

   (d)

   (e)

3. I have been in this job for ______ years.

4. Since I have been in this job it has changed in these ways:

(a)

(b)

(c)

(d)

(e)

5. I enjoy this job for these reasons:

(a)

(b)

(c)

(d)

(e)

6. I dislike this job for these reasons:

(a)

(b)

(c)

(d)

(e)

7. The job is developing the following new competencies in me:

   (a)

   (b)

   (c)

   (d)

   (e)

8. I am not acquiring the following competencies which I probably need for my future career:

   (a)

   (b)

   (c)

   (d)

   (e)

9. This would be a much better job for me if the following would change:

   (a)

   (b)

(c)

(d)

(e)

10. I have taken the following initiatives in the past six months to try to improve my satisfaction with my job:

INITIATIVES	WHAT HAPPENED?
(a)	
(b)	
(c)	
(d)	
(e)	

11. In order to 'shine' at this job I should do the following:

(a)

(b)

(c)

(d)

(e)

12. If I take no new initiatives the job will change in these ways over the next two years:

    (a)

    (b)

    (c)

    (d)

    (e)

13. My job is making a contribution to the wellbeing of others in the following ways:

    (a)

    (b)

    (c)

    (d)

    (e)

14. After reading this chapter I intend to take the following actions (note: re-read the chapter if necessary):

    (a)

    (b)

(c)

(d)

(e)

The final stage . . .

Now you have completed the self-assessment it is necessary to consider the outcome from another perspective. Discuss your current job experience with someone else (if possible your boss). **Then take action!**

Books to Help You Further

Diane Burston (ed.), *An A-Z of Careers and Jobs*, Kogan Page 1984
Awakens minds to possibilities.

Richard Bolles, *What Colour is Your Parachute?*, Umbrella Publishing Services 1985
Great for job seekers – a classic.

Mike Woodcock and Dave Francis, *The Unblocked Manager*, Gower Press 1982
The companion to this book, for managers.

Henry Mintzberg, *The Nature of Managerial Work*, Prentice-Hall 1973
If you want to manage, this book tells you what it is really like.

Edward de Bono, *Opportunities*, Pelican Books 1980
The best visioning book I've found.

Benjamin Tregoe and John Zimmerman, *Top Management Strategy*, John Martin 1980
Too business-orientated for most careerists, but spells out the driving forces concept.

Richard Boyatzis, *The Competent Manager*, John Wiley 1982
Tough going but really important. Expensive, unfortunately.

Robert Townsend, *Up the Organization*, Coronet Books 1971
Good reading and packs a punch.

Gail Sheehy, *Passages: Predictable Crises of Adult Life,* Corgi 1977
Brings genuine insight into the relationship between age and experience.

Ruth Miller and Anna Alston, *Equal Opportunities: a Careers Guide*, Penguin 1978
Useful exploration of issues facing women.

Edgar Schein, *Career Dynamics*, Addison-Wesley 1978
A classic: too academic for some careerists, but it inspired much of the research for this book.

Andrew N. Jones and Cary L. Cooper, *Combating Managerial Obsolescence,* Philip Allan 1980
Introduces important ideas for the middle aged.

Mark H. McCormack, *What They Don't Teach You at Harvard Business School,* Collins 1984
A good debunking book – prospective managers will enjoy it greatly.

David Clutterbuck, *Everyone Needs a Mentor,* IPM Publications 1985
Describes the useful mentor concept in depth.

Alexa Stace and Ruth Sandys, *The Job Finder's Book,* Kogan Page/ Daily Telegraph 1985
If you want to get a job, this will help.

Audrey Segal (ed.), *Careers Encyclopedia,* Cassell 1984
A useful overview with much detail.

Rhona Rappoport and Robert Rappoport, *Working Couples,* Routledge and Kegan Paul 1978
A useful and innovative perspective which will help career planning for pairs.

Muriel James and Dorothy Jongeward, *Born to Win,* Addison-Wesley 1971
Still the most positive self-help book that has ever been written.

Elisabeth Summerson, *Career Information and Career Libraries,* Career Consultants 1984
An overview of resources, especially useful to career counsellors.

Index

Index

ATM is the only voluntary association of professionals in the UK whose work focuses exclusively on management training, education and organization development. Membership is open to anyone involved in this significant field of work. ATM's fast growth in recent years has created a lively membership of interested people in business, government, voluntary organization, academic institutions and management consultancy.

The main aim of ATM is to promote high standards of management performance so that people in organizations and communities can work with greater effectiveness. Members are therefore encouraged to meet and collaborate to improve their own professional capabilities. Activities include evening and one-day meetings, and three- to four-day events held all over the UK and in Europe. These are designed to provide members with different developmental opportunities for the various stages of their careers. They also enable members to extend their knowledge and skills, to keep in touch with frontier thinking on management, and to exchange ideas and experience.

Free publications are sent to members. These include *MEAD* (*Management Education and Development*), a journal which has three issues a year and contains articles on current management training and development; frequent focus papers on topical issues; and a monthly newsletter.

For further information, contact:

ATM
Polytechnic of Central London
35 Marylebone Road
London
NW1 5LS

01-486 5811 (ex. 259)